Also by Richard Deming

Heroes of the International Red Cross
Man Against Man: Civil Law at Work
Man and Society: Criminal Law at Work
Man and the World: International
    Law at Work
Metric Power: Why and How
    We Are Going Metric
Police Lab at Work
Sleep, Our Unknown Life

WOMEN

THE NEW CRIMINALS

RICHARD DEMING

THOMAS NELSON INC., PUBLISHERS

Nashville   New York

Library of Congress Cataloging in Publication Data

Deming, Richard.
    Women: The New Criminals
    Bibliography: p.
    Includes index.
    1. Female offenders—United States. 2. Delinquent girls—United States. 3. Feminism—United States. I. Title.
HV6046.D36   364.3'74'0973   76–40209
ISBN 0–8407–6513–4

For Norm

Contents

Chapter 1

The Changing Pattern
of Female Criminality

All the following eleven incidents had four things in common.

(1) About fifteen minutes after Pedro Gomez, 65, was seen entering his apartment with a young woman, members of a tenants' patrol to combat crime in the apartment complex heard him scream. Rushing to his apartment, they found him stabbed to death and with his pockets turned out. The young woman had made her escape before they arrived.

(2) Joyce Arlene Luciano, 41, was one of seventeen persons arrested in a roundup of loan sharks.

(3) Sharyn Williams, 24, a mother of two children, and Ethel McCree, 17, were arrested for assault and robbery. Police said they were members of a gang composed of five women in their late teens and early twenties that is alleged to have beaten and robbed twenty-five aged persons over a period of about four months. Two of the victims died. The gang's method of operation was to follow its victims home from supermarkets or banks where they had cashed Social Security checks and attack them on elevators or as they walked into their apartments. Police

said they knew the identity of the other three gang members, but did not release their names.

(4) Three teenage girls were arrested for robbing a middle-aged man in his apartment. Squares and X's had been cut in the victim's back and buttocks with a razor blade.

(5) Two teenage girls were arrested for trying to extort $120 from a 44-year-old man on threat of falsely reporting that he had raped one of them.

(6) Dr. Stella Epstein celebrated her eightieth birthday in the hospital, where she lay with a broken hip suffered when she was attacked in Central Park by a gang of nine thirteen-year-old girls.

(7) Diane McCloud, 19, was arrested for the stabbing death of Deborah Brookes, also 19, a rival for a boyfriend's affections.

(8) Delores Smith, 23, was arrested, along with a male companion, for the street robbery-murder in broad daylight of burglar-alarm salesman Michael Cetra, 47.

(9) Sandra Joy Roth, 31, of Park Avenue, along with five male runners who phoned in bets to her, was arrested as the queen pin of a $58-million-a-year gambling ring that specialized in booking bets on sporting events.

(10) Hattie General, 27, and Pamela Taylor, 19, both mothers, were charged with arson after allegedly setting fire to a house after an argument with the occupant.

(11) Goldie Odom, 46, critically wounded her 75-year-old husband during an argument by shooting him in the stomach at close range with a 12-gauge shotgun.

The first thing these incidents had in common was that they all occurred in New York City. The second was that all involved crimes committed by women. The third was that all eleven crimes are types traditionally classed as "male" crimes. And the fourth thing they had in common was that all occurred during the single month of May 1975.

Actually the New York City police arrested several hundred women during that month, but most of the arrests were either for traditional "female" crimes, such as shoplifting, bad-check passing, and prostitution, or for minor offenses such as disturbing the peace and drug possession. The above eleven were culled from the total number of crimes committed by women during May 1975 because they were "male" crimes.

Although that particular month was chosen at random, it is representative of the changing pattern of female criminality in recent years. It was neither a particularly bad month nor a particularly good one for female crime, but more or less run-of-the-mill.

It is proper to question, however, whether New York City, with its huge population, its ghettos and its enormous drug problem, is a reliable measure of what is happening in other parts of the United States, or in other parts of the world. So let us take a look at a totally dissimilar community clear across the country from New York City.

The city of Oxnard, on the California coast about sixty miles north of Los Angeles, has a population of 87,000. In this relatively quiet suburban community both the general crime rate per thousand of population and the female crime rate are considerably lower than those of New York City. During the month of May 1975 only a few women were arrested for crimes other than shoplifting, bad-check passing, prostitution, and narcotics offenses. But four arrests were definitely "male" crimes.

(1) Two women were arrested for kidnapping.
(2) A woman and two male companions forced their

way into the home of a 75-year-old woman, robbed her, and ransacked the house.

(3) A man-and-woman team held up the cashier of a movie theater.

(4) A woman was arrested as a fence for stolen property.

In all fairness it must be admitted that this was not an average month for Oxnard. With so much less crime than New York City, the month-to-month fluctuation there is greater than in the larger community. A more representative month was December 1975, when there were only half as many "male" crimes committed by women as in May.

(1) Deciderio Rubalcaba, 71, let a woman who said she had auto trouble into his home to make a phone call. The woman in turn admitted two men, one of whom held the victim at knife point while she and the other man took Rubalcaba's wallet and ransacked his house. A few days later Augustine Tridado, 66, told police that a woman came to the door of his home to ask for a drink of water. Spotting two men hiding alongside the door, he slammed and locked it, but they broke it open and held knives to his ribs while the woman ransacked the house. On December 13 police arrested Manuela "Nellie" Hinjosa, 19, the mother of an infant, and two male companions for those two crimes and a dozen similar previous robberies.

(2) A tavern owner awakened in the middle of the night to find three women in his bedroom, going through his dresser drawers. They fled when challenged, but shortly afterward police stopped a car in the area containing five women, three of whom the victim later identified as the burglars. Lynn Barnett, 25, Retia Gayle Stewart, 23, and

Betty Banks, 34, were booked on burglary and conspiracy charges. Lynn Barnett and one of the other women in the car, Judy Taylor, 27, already faced robbery charges, previously filed, for the alleged robbery of a businessman of $3,155.

Here are a few other incidents, chosen at random, which occurred in various parts of the country in recent years:

(1) In Detroit a 31-year-old female street mugger bashed a 62-year-old man with a length of metal pipe and escaped with his wallet.

(2) In Buffalo a 26-year-old woman killed her lover and his two small sons, then barricaded herself in and shot it out with twenty policemen for three hours. Finally, instead of giving up, she killed herself.

(3) Three prominent men were victims of female assailants who were strangers to them in separate incidents in Manhattan. Franz Josef Strauss, former defense minister of West Germany, was mugged by three women on Fifth Avenue. Pasquale Bottero, an Italian glass manufacturer, was stabbed to death on the street by a female robber. Charles Addams, the noted cartoonist, had acid thrown on the back of his neck by two prostitutes who became angry when he ignored them.

(4) A teenage girl told the desk clerk of a New Orleans motel (if he didn't empty the cash register), "I am going to spill your guts." When he refused, she stepped behind the counter and stabbed him. As she was taking the money, three motel guests separately approached the desk, where the bleeding clerk lay out of sight on the floor behind the counter. The female robber calmly made change for the first, gave the second his room key, and checked out the third. Then she strolled out with the stolen money.

Uniform Crime Reports is the title of a thick annual book of nearly three hundred pages issued by the Federal Bureau of Investigation. It is a compilation and analysis of data submitted by police organizations from all over the country. Because I have made extensive use of FBI statistics in this book, it is important to establish their validity, so I will go into the methods used in collecting data in some detail.

The problems connected with collecting accurate data are enormous. For one thing, all fifty states have differing definitions of many crimes, so that an act defined as burglary in one state may be only theft or larceny in another. Furthermore reports come from one-man police departments in rural areas, big-city police departments with computerized record keeping, and police agencies of every size in between. Some agencies neglect to submit reports, so that figures are never 100 percent comprehensive.

The FBI does the best it can to minimize the effect of these problems. In order to keep reporting procedures from all submitting agencies as similar as possible, it stipulates the crimes to be reported, and gives detailed definitions of each. Crimes are divided into Part I and Part II offenses, with Part I being the more serious crimes.

There are seven Part I offenses: (1) criminal homicide, (2) forcible rape, (3) robbery, (4) aggravated assault, (5) burglary—breaking or entering, (6) larceny—theft (except motor-vehicle theft), (7) motor-vehicle theft.

There are twenty-two Part II offenses, which include such things as simple assault, fraud, embezzlement, and the various so-called victimless crimes, such as prostitution, gambling, and narcotics offenses. Each is defined in detail, so that reports will reflect the same types of crimes even when local definitions vary.

For example, the FBI definition of robbery is: *Stealing or taking anything of value from the care, custody, or control of a person by force or violence or by putting in fear, such as strong-arm robbery, stickups, armed robbery, assaults to rob, and attempts to rob.* The fifty states each have their own definitions of robbery, but in reporting to the FBI, agencies are expected to report as robberies only those crimes falling within the FBI definition.

It is said that anything can be proved by statistics. Though that may be true, it is also true that statistical studies can be highly accurate when data are scientifically compiled and evaluated. In recent years the television networks have been able to predict the outcomes of elections with amazing accuracy when less than 5 percent of returns are in by running data from key spots through computers. FBI statistics represent returns from the majority of police agencies throughout the country. The latest report, issued on August 25, 1976, covering the year 1975, represents 95 percent of the national population. Thus, though they are hardly infallible, FBI statistics probably reflect trends with considerable accuracy.

Having stipulated that these statistics are not infallible, I will hereafter cite them as though they were, simply to avoid the necessity of repeatedly qualifying them by explaining that they represent returns from only 85 percent, or 90 percent, or whatever, of all the police agencies asked for data. It should therefore be kept in mind that when a statistic—such as the numbers of crimes committed by women in 1960 and 1975—is quoted, this statistic represents merely the numbers of arrests *reported*, and the total figures would be higher if all police agencies that were asked to submit reports had done so.

During the decade from 1960 to 1970, arrests of men for major (Part I) crimes rose 25.7 percent. Arrests of women rose 74.4 percent, or nearly three times the rate of increase for men during the same period.

For a number of reasons the sharp growth of female crime attracted little attention. For one thing, men were still committing the vast majority of crimes, so that the numerical growth of men's crimes still was greater than the numerical growth of women's crimes. In actual numbers major crimes of women grew from 387,073 in 1960 to 675,212 in 1970, for an increase of only approximately 288,000 crimes, spread through all fifty states with a total population of more than 200 million. For another thing the radical movement of the 1960's and the increasing violence of the civil-rights movement directed popular attention away from this relatively minor matter. For a third, the general public tends not to become aware of profound social change until it is so well underway that it can no longer go unnoticed.

In illustration of this last point, one criterion of public awareness of issues is what is being written about them. Let us look at what Americans have been reading about female crime in recent years.

The *Reader's Guide to Periodical Literature* is a comprehensive index of magazine articles published in all major American periodicals. In the six-year period from the beginning of 1970 to the end of 1975 there were 26 articles on women shoplifters and 31 on prostitution, the two most frequent traditional female crimes. There were 17 on girl delinquents, 10 of them concerned solely with runaways. Despite the increase in major crimes by women during the 1960's, and their progressively greater increase ever since, no magazine articles on the subject appeared until 1972, when one was printed. None appeared in 1973, three were published in 1974, and six in 1975.

Apparently the public is belatedly becoming aware that society has a brand-new problem.

In indication of the size of the problem, by the end of 1975 major crimes by males had increased over the 1960 rate by 119.3 percent, major crimes by females had increased by 373.5 percent. The rate of increase by males under 18 was 117.4 percent, by females under 18 it was 425.4 percent.

As yet men still commit most of the crimes, even though the gap is steadily closing. Male arrests outnumbered female arrests by five to one in 1975, and only one out of ten arrested for violent crimes was a woman. But the increase in male arrests over 1974 was only 2 percent, whereas it was 4 percent for women. The increase in violent crimes by women over 1974 was 5 percent.

Obviously if the same pattern continues, we will soon reach a point when crimes committed by women equal or even exceed the number committed by men.

On Christmas Day 1975 the *Los Angles Times* published a feature article on the women who had made national headlines during 1975. Six of the women listed had made headlines because of violent crimes.

The jump in female crime is not confined to the United States, although it seems to be larger here than anywhere else in the world. Dr. Gerhard O. W. Mueller, chief of the United Nations Crime Prevention and Criminal Justice Section, says, "Female criminality in all categories is rising between three and five times as fast as male criminality in the advanced countries."

What Dr. Mueller means by "advanced countries" he doesn't make clear, but presumably he means the industrially developed nations. Except for the United States and Great Britain, statistical evidence doesn't seem to bear out Dr. Mueller's statement.

In Britain between 1968 and 1974 major offenses by men rose 25 percent, by women, 54 percent. Crimes of violence by British women more than doubled during that period. In several boroughs of London roving bands of female muggers, called "granny bashers" because of their tendency to pick elderly women as victims, terrorized whole areas. In Northern Ireland, since the revolutionist Irish Republican Army first admitted women in 1970, women have taken an increasingly active part in terrorist activity. More than half the members of the revolutionary organization called The Angry Brigade, now believed broken up, were estimated to have been women.

In Japan there was a 22 percent rise in female crime over the past five years. But despite this statistic, Japan has no appreciable female crime problem. Though the number of female crimes steadily grows, the percentage of crimes committed by women is still negligible, and most of the 22 percent increase is due to minor crimes. The exception is political terrorism. The revolutionist Red Army has a large female membership, and three of the eight persons arrested in December 1975 for a number of political bombings were women.

In West Germany there has been no appreciable increase in ordinary crimes by women, but female political terrorists are steadily increasing in number there too. Of the twenty-six members of the now disbanded Baader-Meinhof gang, a terrorist group committed to violence as a device to bring about social change, ten were women.

In Canada female crime has more than doubled over the past twenty-five years, but it is still not a serious problem. Only about 10 percent of all crimes in Canada are committed by women.

In Spain, France, Italy, and Switzerland there has been little change in the rates of crime by women in recent years, other than in terrorist activity. In Spain and Italy women rarely commit crimes, possibly because both countries are still male-dominated societies where most women are kept mainly in the status of homemakers and mothers.

In France there was a 2.6 percent drop in female crime from 1973 to 1974, which State Secretary for Women's Affairs Françoise Giroud explains as largely the result of enlightened legislation concerning women. By law women must be paid the same wages as men for similar work. In addition, working women are provided with nurseries for their small children, and laws concerning abortion, birth control, and divorce have either been liberalized or are in the process of being liberalized. As a result, Secretary Giroud says, "Women's Liberation in France has not become the aggressive element it is in the United States." Though this is no doubt partially true, the secretary's explanation seems oversimplified.

In Switzerland female crime has risen only 1 percent in ten years.

Terrorism by women in both Spain and Italy is on the rise, though. In Spain the two most active revolutionary groups, the Basque Land and Liberty Army and the Patriotic Revolutionary Antifascist Front, both contain women. In Italy terrorist Margherita Cagol of the revolutionary Red Brigade died in a gunfight with police in 1975.

No crime figures are released by Communist countries, but periodic reports of crimes by women seep from Moscow. Three 1975 cases reported from there involved the theft by a woman of goods worth more than $50,000 from a department store, a woman engineer who fraudulently collected awards for nonexistent technological accomplishments, and a woman plant manager who stole material worth more than $30,000 from her plant.

One type of crime that except for a few isolated cases has always been overwhelmingly a male crime is political assassination. Women have murdered a sizable number of political leaders for reasons other than political, but crimes of passion are not political assassinations, even when the victims are heads of state. When the mistress of a king or prince stabs her lover in a jealous rage, she is merely a murderess, not an assassin, regardless of the political consequences of her act. Assassination as an act of political protest is something quite different. Usually it is committed because of the assassin's belief in some cause, and more often than not the killer is unknown to the victim.

There have been a few female assassins and would-be assassins, though. One of the earliest is recorded in the Old Testament in Judges 4:17–22.

Somewhere about 1100 or 1200 B.C., in a war between Canaan and Israel, the Israelites defeated and routed the Canaanite army at the River Kishon near Kedesh. Sisera, commander of the Canaanite army, fled for protection to the tent of Heber the Kenite on a plain near Kedesh. The Kenites were a Canaanite tribe friendly to the Israelites, and they disapproved of the war, but Heber had severed his ties with his own people and was politically on the side of Canaan's King Jabin. Although Sisera was unaware of it, Heber's wife Jael differed with her husband's political philosophy, and was militantly pro-Israel. Heber was away when Sisera arrived. Jael welcomed the Canaanite, fixed him a bed, gave him some goat's milk, and then, when Sisera had fallen asleep, assassinated him with typical Old Testament brutality by nailing his head to the earthen floor with a tent stake.

In 1793 Marie Anne Charlotte Corday d'Armont, more commonly known simply as Charlotte Corday, stuck a kitchen knife though the heart of Jean Paul Marat, an important leader of the French Revolution, and was guillotined for the act. On June 28, 1914, the same day on which a student radical in Bosnia set off World War I by assassinating Archduke Francis Ferdinand of the Austro-Hungarian Empire and his wife Sophie, a peasant woman in Pokrovskoe, Siberia, stabbed, but failed to kill, the notorious "mad monk" Grigori Efimovich Rasputin. In 1918 Fanya Kaplan put two bullets in Nikolai Lenin, the father of the Russian Revolution, but he, too, survived.

Up until September 1975, female political assassins were unknown in the United States. A woman had been among the four hanged for conspiracy in the assassination plot against Abraham Lincoln, Vice President Andrew Johnson, and Secretary of State William Seward, but Mary Surratt had taken no part in the actual assassination of the President or the attempted assassinations of the other two, and there is some doubt that she was even guilty of conspiracy. The main evidence at her trial was merely that the conspirators had hatched the plot at her boardinghouse.

Then in September 1975, within two weeks of each other, Lynette Alice (Squeaky) Fromme, 26, and Sara Jane Moore, 45, attempted to assassinate President Gerald Ford. Women had finally graduated even to the uniquely male crime of political assassination.

Violent crimes by women tend to upset ordinary people more than violent crimes by men, because traditionally women are softer, gentler creatures. The general attitude toward the new criminality among women was succinctly expressed by the title of a 1969 book by Edith de Rham, which recounts the exploits of a number of female criminals of the past. The title was *How Could She Do That?*

Chapter 2

The Myth of Feminine Nonviolence

In Chapter 5, where the causes of the rise in female criminality will be discussed, it will be shown that there is considerable disagreement among experts. But one thing most have come to agree about is that the traditional concept that women are less prone to violence than men is a myth. Dr. Leon Salzman of the Albert Einstein College of Medicine pretty well summed up current thinking by sociologists, psychologists, and anthropologists when he said, "There is no biological reason for the female to be less aggressive than the male. It's just that being aggressive had no meaning in a woman's life until she had the possibilities that a man does."

Experts in all three fields generally now concur that women traditionally have acted less aggressively than men simply because of cultural pressures. For thousands of years it has been drilled into daughters that "nice" girls behave in a ladylike manner, and it has been drilled into sons that "manly" behavior is expected of them. Let a little girl get into a fight, and both parents are distressed. When a little boy gets into one, the mother may be distressed, but all too often the father's main interest is merely whether or not his son won. The well-known nursery rhyme telling us that little boys are made of "frogs and snails and puppy dog tails" and little girls of "sugar and spice and all that's nice" is more than mere whimsy; it constitutes a basic cultural belief.

I recall as a child my older brother, who was about ten at the time, coming home crying because a playmate had taken his favorite shooting marble from him. Instead of handling the matter on a parental level, my father instructed my brother to go get the marbel back, and not to return without it. When Fred returned with a black eye, but triumphantly clutching the marble, he was greeted with a proud hug.

I had no sisters, but I am quite sure that if I had had one, and some item had been taken from her by a playmate, it would not even have occurred to my father to handle the matter that way. My mother would have handled it by informing the other girl's mother of the theft.

Among predatory animals females are no less aggressive than males. A lioness is just as dangerous game as a lion, and she is more dangerous when defending her young. A cornered female wolf will go for your throat as quickly as a male wolf. Both the vixen and the fox are hunters. It would be strange if among humans, the most predatory of all animals, only males were genetically capable of violence.

Over the ages a few poets, philosophers, and social commentators have dropped occasional hints that women are not necessarily as gentle-natured as myth would have us believe. Ecclesiasticus 25:19 says, "All wickedness is but little to the wickedness of a woman." Around 800 B.C. the ancient Greek poet Homer said, "There is no fouler fiend than a woman when her mind is bent to evil." Five hundred years later Menander, a Greek writer of comedies, said, "Of all the wild beasts on land or sea, the wildest is woman." About 50 B.C. the Roman writer Pub-lilius Syrus said, "In evil counsel women always beat men." Napoleon Bonaparte told an interviewer on the island of St. Helena, where he was exiled, in 1817, "Women, when they are bad, are worse than men, and more ready to commit crimes." And, of course, there is the best-known quote of all on the subject, by Rudyard Kipling, "The female of the species is more deadly than the male."

The evidence supporting these opinions has been there all along. Although it is true that there has always been a much smaller number of female criminals than male ones, for reasons which will be discussed in a later chapter, when women did commit crimes, they could be just as fiendish as the worst of men. Among the "gentler sex" there has even been an impressive number of monsters.

A seventeenth-century Neapolitan woman named Toffana peddled a "cosmetic lotion" with an arsenic base which she generally labeled Aqua Toffana, but which she also sold under a couple of other names. Although she publicly promoted the concoction as effective for removing skin blemishes, Toffana quietly let her wealthy women clients know it was also good for removing unwanted husbands or lovers. Toffana is believed to have murdered some six hundred people with her lotion at second hand.

A contemporary of Toffana in France was Marie Madeleine Marguerite d'Aubray, the beautiful and charming wife of Antoine, the Marquis de Brinvilliers. In 1660, when she was twenty-nine, after eight years of marriage, the marquise openly took a lover, a cavalry officer called Sainte-Croix. The marquis had no objection to this, since he had several mistresses himself. As a matter of fact he had introduced Sainte-Croix, who was a friend of his, to his wife in the hope she would become preoccupied enough with the dashing cavalry officer to let him follow his own amatory pursuits. Marie's father, who was Treasurer of France, was horrified at his daughter's scandalous behavior, though, and was politically powerful enough to have her lover thrown into the Bastille on a trumped-up charge. It took Marie six months of string-pulling among her own influential friends to get him out.

One of the most-heard criticisms of modern prisons is that instead of rehabilitating criminals, they tend to be schools for crime. That same criticism could be leveled at the Bastille of the seventeenth century. Sainte-Croix's cellmate was an Italian poisoner named Exili, and from him Marie's lover learned more about poisons than most apothecaries knew.

Marie was running short of money when Sainte-Croix was finally released, and the cavalry officer had never had any. They decided the quickest way to get some was to hasten Marie's inheritance.

At this point the Marquise de Brinvilliers began to exhibit the casual attitude toward murder that distinguishes the monster from the ordinary killer. In order to test the relative effectiveness of the various poisons concocted by her lover, she began making charitable visits to Paris hospitals, carrying baskets of fruit to needy patients. It is not known just how many invalids succumbed to her scientific curiosity, because in her eventual confession Marie said she couldn't recall, but she did make it clear that she had conducted a thorough experiment.

In 1666 Marie went to stay with her father for a time in order to nurse him over a minor illness. His illness quickly worsened, and eventually he died. Only a fourth of his fortune went to Marie, though, because she had two younger brothers and a younger sister. In 1667 she partially undid that injustice by poisoning her two brothers, whose shares of the family fortune then went to Marie and her sister.

Before polishing off her sister, Marie decided to tidy up her domestic affairs by disposing of her husband so that she could marry Sainte-Croix. But the cavalry officer had no desire to marry her, and besides that, the Marquis de Brinvilliers was his friend. It was revealed among his papers after his death that on several occasions after Marie confided to him that she had given poison to her husband, Sainte-Croix rushed to administer antidotes.

Eventually Marie must have decided her husband was immune to her poisons, because she gave up further attempts and turned her attention to her sister. But before she could poison her, Sainte-Croix unexpectedly died, apparently of natural causes, leaving behind a red oblong box packed with incriminating letters from Marie, the recipes for the poisons used, some samples of the poisons, and a list of the antidotes he had administered to Marie's husband. When she heard of her lover's death, Marie rushed to his rooms to get the box, but the police had already carried it off.

She fled to the Netherlands, where she hid out in a convent for three years, but eventually was brought back to Paris to stand trial and be convicted. She was beheaded in 1676, at the age of forty-six.

Four years later a Paris counterpart of Toffana known as La Voisin (her real name was Catherine Deshayes) was burned at the stake for the secondhand murders of countless victims to whose murderers she had sold poisons, and for the actual murders of numerous unwanted children brought to her for disposal. What makes La Voisin particularly monstrous is that, despite her horrible specialty, she was a doting mother to her own children.

A few other female monsters chosen at random are: Anna Zwanziger, a huge, grossly unattractive Bavarian woman arrested in 1809 for poisoning a number of young brides, her motive having been to increase the number of eligible men in her locality, in the hope of catching a husband herself; Mary Ann Cotton of England, who between 1853 and 1874 poisoned twenty-four people, including a number of her own children; a Dutch woman named Van der Linden, who between 1869 and 1885 murdered twenty-seven by poison and made seventy-five other unsuccessful attempts to poison people.

The two women probably best known for their monstrousness don't deserve their evil reputations. Historians now believe that Lucrezia Borgia not only never poisoned anyone, but that she was a particularly kindly and pious woman. There is considerable evidence that her father, who later became Pope Alexander VI, and her brother Cesare each murdered a number of people, but apparently Lucrezia was party to none of the murders. Cesare also arranged a number of murders he didn't personally commit, including the murders of his and Lucrezia's brother Juan and of Lucrezia's first husband, Alfonso of Aragon. Lucrezia was grief-stricken by both deaths, and almost certainly was unaware of Cesare's complicity in either. Her evil reputation developed from enemies of the Borgia family who spread stories that she was a poisoner like her father and brother.

The other probably undeserved reputation is that of Lizzie Borden. Her name summons an automatic picture of a young woman hacking her father and stepmother to death with an ax, but she was acquitted of the charge, and at least some authorities who have studied her case in depth are convinced she actually was innocent.

America has had its share of bona-fide female monsters, though.

In the early 1900's Belle Gunness, a widow living on a farm near La Porte, Indiana, began advertising for husbands in lonely-hearts columns. She had already lost two husbands in suspicious accidents, and in other parts of the country had twice collected insurance for fires where arson was suspected but couldn't be proved. A whole array of lonely men answered her ads, appeared at the farm long enough to transfer their assets to Belle, then disappeared again. Her total score is estimated to have been around twenty murders, although only fourteen bodies were discovered buried on her farm when an investigation was finally made in 1908.

Belle was tipped off by a hired hand, who was also an occasional lover, that the investigation was coming. The farmhouse burned down while the sheriff was en route to question her. Among the ruins were found the charred remains of Belle's three children and a headless female body wearing Belle's rings on the fingers. Strangely the fire seemed to have shrunken Belle, if it was Belle, because the corpse was of average size and Belle weighed 280 pounds. It was never proved to be anyone else's body, though, and no one of Belle's description was ever again seen in the area.

There have been numerous other mass murderesses in American history, but my favorite monster is Nannie Doss, the giggling killer of eleven who confessed to her crimes with the wide-eyed innocence of a small girl admitting she had been in the cookie jar. Nannie, nicknamed Arsenic Annie by the press, practiced her lethal art over a period of almost thirty years before she was finally caught.

In October 1954, in Tulsa, Oklahoma, Samuel Doss was released from the hospital, where he had been under treatment for stomach pains. He died the next day. The attending physician, Dr. N. Z. Schwelbein, thought there ought to be an autopsy. The widow, a plump, spectacled woman of forty-nine, nine years younger than the deceased, agreed. "Whatever he had might kill somebody else," she told the doctor. "It's best to find out."

Why she so readily agreed is a mystery to this day, because what was found out was that the body contained enough arsenic to kill an elephant. Nannie was amazed when the police informed her. "How could that be?" she inquired with wide-eyed innocence. "All I fed him when he came home from the hospital was a dish of stewed prunes, and there was certainly no arsenic in that."

She was one of the most agreeably cooperative suspects the Tulsa police had ever questioned. Her answers were so voluble that they kept having to interrupt to get in the next question. Her coy, little-girl manner struck them as a bit outlandish in a middle-aged grandmother, but her innocent air seemed so unassumed that they began to believe she was innocent. Then one of the policemen who had done a little research asked a question about the untimely death of Richard Morton about a year and a half earlier. Nannie said she had never heard of him.

Staring at her in disbelief, the policeman said, "You don't remember your previous husband?"

Nannie giggled. "Oh, *that* Richard Morton. Yes, I was married to him."

In those days, before the Escobedo and Miranda Supreme Court decisions, a suspect could be questioned more or less indefinitely, and the police were permitted to employ all sorts of since barred devices, such as leading questions and lies about what evidence they had, to trick the suspect into a confession. In *Escobedo v. Illinois* in 1964 the United States Supreme Court granted suspects the right to have a lawyer present during interrogation, even before charges are preferred. *Miranda v. Arizona* in 1966 affirmed the previous decision and added that the suspect must be informed of the right to have a lawyer and must be furnished one at public expense if he is unable to afford to hire one. In 1954 the police were burdened by no such restrictions, however. Nannie was questioned nonstop for several days before she finally broke down and admitted she had poisoned both Samuel Doss and Richard Morton.

When news of the confession hit the wire services, the Tulsa police began to receive inquiries from other police departments. Of Nannie's five husbands, it developed that four had died after being seized by stomach pains. Number one, whom she had married at age fifteen, had escaped that fate by divorcing her, but only after two of their children had died with stomach pains. A third child, a daughter, managed to survive, grow up, and eventually have children of her own.

A two-year-old grandson of one of her husbands and the young nephew of another had also died under similar circumstances. Then it was discovered that Nannie's mother and two sisters had died in the same way. Police all over the country began getting court orders to dig up bodies. Altogether eleven, including the two Tulsa husbands, were found to be full of arsenic.

Throughout her trial Nannie Doss retained her bright, jolly air. One news photo shows her in the hallway of the Tulsa courthouse, laughing gaily at her surviving daughter, and with her arms about her two granddaughters. Her daughter's expression appears a little stunned, but the two granddaughters, both quite young, are smiling broadly.

Nannie's motive for the murders of her four husbands was simply that she was romantic, she explained. All her life she had been searching for romance of the same quality she read about in her favorite magazine, *True Romances*. But every one of her husbands had been boring, and though she had made a little insurance profit from each, her main motive had merely been to get them out of the way so that she could search for a more meaningful relationship.

She never explained why she had also killed her mother, two sisters, and four children, two of them her own. Sentenced to life imprisonment, Nannie Doss died of leukemia in prison in 1965, giggling almost up until her final coma.

There have probably been as many male as female monsters, or perhaps even more. It is difficult to judge, because the compilation of crime statistics is still relatively recent. The FBI's Uniform Crime Reporting Program didn't begin until 1930, and it was some years after that before enough bugs were ironed out to make it an accurate reflection of the nation's crime picture.

You get the impression from what crime records have survived in history that neither sex has a corner on cruelty, though. Probably Rudyard Kipling would have stated it more accurately if he had said, "The female of the species is just as deadly as the male."

Chapter 3

"Male" Crimes by Women of the Past

Traditionally poisoning has been classed as a "woman's crime," not because there have been more women than men who killed by that method, but mainly because prior to the twentieth century women committed so few other serious crimes compared to men that their poisonings stuck out glaringly. We are concerned primarily with the growing number of "male" crimes committed by women, however. And when you search for those in the past, the rate of female criminality shrinks drastically.

During every period of history there have always been some women who committed male crimes, though. There have been highwaywomen, female embezzlers, thieves, con-artists, kidnappers—even female pirates.

One of the most famous pirates of the West Indies was Anne Bonny, a strapping but beautiful redhead who went into battle wearing black velvet trousers, a crimson blouse, and a wide belt holding a brace of pistols and a rapier. Born in 1700, Anne was the daughter of a Charleston, South Carolina, businessman named William Cormac, who made a fortune dealing with pirates. She was tutored in the usual ladylike subjects of French, music, and art, but on the side she managed to get lessons in more interesting subjects by two men who worked for her father—a fencing instructor and an Indian named Charlie Fourfeathers. By the time she was ten she was expert with the rapier, could handle a musket and a pistol like a man, and could split an apple with either a knife or tomahawk at fifteen paces.

To say Anne was a tomboy would be an understatement. At thirteen she killed a woman in a knife fight and had to appear before a coroner's jury. The jury voted self-defense.

At that time piracy was a somewhat tolerated crime. Even respectable merchants felt justified in dealing with pirates because of England's restrictive trade and tax laws. So long as pirates preyed only on French and Spanish shipping, the Royal Navy tended to look the other way. A pirate's social status was equivalent to that of a bootlegger in the 1920's. He wasn't quite respectable, but he wasn't exactly a criminal either. A number of pirates had offices on the Charleston waterfront, where they sold their plunder to merchants such as William Cormac. Through her father Anne came to know many of them. That was how she met James Bonny, a minor pirate and petty smuggler.

Over her parents' violent objections she married Bonny when she was sixteen. The shock killed her mother and caused her father to disown her. Anne sailed away with her new husband to a settlement of pirates at New Providence in the Bahamas.

Her entrance into the pirate community was spectacular. By age sixteen she had attained her full growth, and was a buxom, imposing woman only an inch or two under six feet tall. As she, her husband, and the pirate crew of the ship they had arrived on started toward town from the harbor, a huge, one-eared pirate blocked Anne's way and informed her the toll for passing was a kiss. Anne calmly drew a pistol and shot off his other ear.

The incident not only made her instantly famous throughout the island, but won her acceptance by the pirates as an equal. Quickly tiring of James Bonny, she became the mistress of Chidley Bayard, the wealthiest man on the island. She had to kill Bayard's current mistress in a duel first, but once that minor matter was settled, she moved into Bayard's mansion and told her husband to get lost.

Anne moved on from Bayard to become the mistress of several pirate captains, and to sail with them as a ship's officer. Eventually she became captain of her own ship, the *Queen Royal*, and she had a female mate named Mary Read serving under her. The *Queen Royal* took numerous prizes, and Anne was a popular captain. (She had to be, since pirate captains were elected by the crews.) She was a strict disciplinarian and insisted that her men bathe regularly. There is a legend that she once refused to let the infamous Captain Edward Teach, better known as Blackbeard the Pirate, aboard her ship until he had taken a bath, something he hadn't done in fifteen years.

In one matter her discipline was somewhat lax, and that was her undoing. She permitted her crew to drink aboard ship after taking a prize. In October 1720 a Royal Navy sloop sneaked up alongside the *Queen Royal* when everyone aboard was drunk except Anne, Mary Read, and one sailor. The sober sailor was killed by the boarders, but there were no other casualties. Anne and Mary were overpowered, and the drunken crew was disarmed without trouble. Anne was twenty years old.

About a year before, the official policy of ignoring pirates had suddenly ended, mainly because they were no longer confining themselves to Spanish and French prizes, but were also attacking British ships. Woodes Rogers, governor of the Bahamas, had offered amnesty to all pirates who would lay down their arms. About six hundred had accepted, but Anne was one of the holdouts. When the *Queen Royal* was brought into port, there was some public clamor to extend the now expired amnesty to cover at least the two women. When Mary Read died in her cell while awaiting trial, largely of neglect, the clamor grew. The governor gave in. Anne was pardoned on condition she leave the West Indies and never return.

Meantime James Bonny had died, freeing Anne to re-marry. She married her latest lover, Michael Ratcliffe, a pirate who had accepted the original amnesty terms. The last anyone heard of the pair, they were heading west from Norfolk, Virginia, in a wagon train, to find free land on the frontier.

In 1733 in London there occurred such a brutal robbery-murder that it was automatically assumed a man had committed the crime. Three women were found mur-dered in their beds in a flat in Tanfield Court. Elderly Mrs. Lydia Duncomb, a widow, and sixty-year-old Betty Har-rison, her nurse-companion, had been strangled. A seventeen-year-old maid named Ann Price had had her throat cut. A strongbox at the foot of Mrs. Duncomb's bed, forced open and empty, was the obvious motive for the crime.

The criminal arrested, convicted, and hanged was a pretty young charwoman named Sarah Malcolm.

At least three stagecoach robbers of the Old West were women, but none of them was very good at the trade.

In 1858 a hard-drinking female professional gambler known only as Dutch Kate, along with two male compan-ions, attempted to recoup a recent disastrous poker loss by holding up the Wells Fargo stage a few miles outside Forest City, California. Unfortunately for Kate, driver Wil-liam Wilson had played poker with her and recognized her as the leader of the trio by her voice, despite her being masked and dressed in men's clothing. Unfortunately for all three robbers, Kate had gotten her dates mixed. She had learned that a shipment of gold was coming in on the stage, but she had picked the wrong day. The strongbox was empty.

Kate allowed the stage to continue on without thinking to search the passengers. If she read the eventual newspaper account of the robbery, it must have upset her to learn one of the passengers had been carrying $15,000 in gold. She may never have seen the report, though. Realizing she was recognized because the stagecoach driver had called her by name, she disappeared from the area and was never heard of again. Her two male confederates were never identified.

In 1874 sixteen-year-old Elizabeth Keith held up the same stage two days in a row at the same spot outside of Sonora, California. The first time she and her companion, Fred Wilson, got a mine payroll. Rightly guessing that the stolen payroll would have to be replaced and would be on the next day's stage, they decided to get it, too.

Unfortunately for the robbers, the driver had his blacksnake whip in his hand when they ordered him to halt, and stage drivers could do miraculous things with their long whips. The driver reined the horses to a halt, but then the whip lashed out, cracked against the forehead of Fred Wilson, knocking him down, then wound around the girl's neck and jerked her off her feet. The driver and a passenger riding on top with him jumped down to grab the robbers' guns before they could recover.

Both robbers got prison terms.

The most famous female stagecoach robber was Pearl Hart, but her fame stemmed from her public performances rather than from her exploits as an outlaw. In 1899, when she was twenty-eight, Pearl and her lover, Joe Boot, held up a stage between Globe and Florence, Arizona. Their loot was $500. Two days later a posse found them camped by a river, peacefully sleeping.

Returned to Florence to be jailed, they were met by a large crowd curious to see "the lady stage robber." Pearl gave them their money's worth. She made a speech in which she explained that she had a dying mother in Ontario, Canada, and she had robbed the stage in order to send her mother money for medical attention. When reporters checking out the story discovered she really did have a dying mother in Ontario, and that she had previously sent her mother money for hospital bills, sob sisters latched on to the story and made Pearl a cause célèbre.

The story had begun to fade from the news when Pearl was transferred to the Tucson jail to await trial. She got in the headlines again by escaping from jail. Again she had faded from the news when, months later, she was captured in New Mexico in the midst of organizing a gang to rob stagecoaches, with herself as the leader. Her capture took place before the gang actually began operations, so no new charges were filed against her, but there was considerable publicity about "the lady gang leader."

Back in the Tucson jail, Pearl garnered still more publicity by declaring she was the victim of discrimination because she was charged under a law passed by a legislature composed entirely of men, without women even being consulted. She called on the women of Arizona Territory to demand equal rights in lawmaking.

This preposterous defense actually worked. Or perhaps it was the story of the dying mother. The jury, all male, didn't explain how it arrived at its verdict of not guilty.

The judge, outraged at the verdict, ordered a second trial on the charge of stealing a pistol from the stagecoach driver. Today there is little doubt that this charge would have been dismissed as double jeopardy, but Pearl was retried, convicted, and sentenced to five years, of which she served three.

Joe Boot, less lucky, was convicted of stagecoach robbery on the same evidence upon which Pearl had been acquitted, and drew thirty years.

During the 1930's there was an unprecedented spate of gun-toting female criminals. Just to mention a few, in 1931 two-hundred-pound Margaret Sherman was arrested by Chicago police after committing more than one hundred armed robberies with a .38 caliber pistol. That same year bank robber Gladys Carlson was executed for the murder of two policemen. In 1934 the most famous female bandit of the era, Bonnie Parker of Bonnie-and-Clyde fame, died in a hail of machine-gun bullets after a two-year spree of bank robberies. In 1935 Ma Barker, head of the infamous Karpis-Barker gang, which under her guidance had robbed at least fourteen banks and had pulled three kidnappings for ransom, died in a blazing gun battle with FBI agents.

Numerous causes combined to produce this new type of female criminal. One was that the flapper era of the 1920's, which had just ended, had released women from a lot of age-old restrictions on their behavior. Though it was a giant step from carrying a flask on your hip to carrying a gun there, it wasn't any more giant than the step from the pre-World-War-I hobble skirt to the hip flask. Women whose mothers had concealed even their ankles wore dresses halfway up their thighs. Demure, ladylike girls sat home, waiting for the phone to ring, while the flappers were out having fun. A totally different type of behavior by women was suddenly permitted, and this attitude carried over into the underworld. Though the general public was shocked by the new gunwomen, their behavior was accepted, and even admired, *within their own peer group.* Gladys Carlson's husband Carl, who was her partner in bank robberies, was inordinately proud of the way she handled a gun. So was Clyde Barrow proud of Bonnie's expertise. Bank robber Alvin Karpis had such a mother complex about Ma Barker that he mailed a letter to J. Edgar Hoover threatening to kill him after G-Men killed her.

A second factor that caused the emergence of the female criminal was the depression. With college graduates standing on street corners selling apples, it was virtually impossible for anyone lacking education and skills to get even the most menial job. And most of the bandits of that era, both male and female, fell into that category. Simple inability to make money any other way drove many into crime.

Probably the largest reason for the increase of female bandits was simply that banditry in general increased during the 1930's. This was the era of the bank robbers, when outlaws such as John Dillinger, Pretty Boy Floyd, and Baby Face Nelson ran the police ragged. Police forces were so poorly trained and inadequate at that time that these criminals were able to flourish—for a time—almost openly. Deadly marksmen, often armed with submachine guns, they time and again blasted their way past policemen carrying only rusty pistols. Even when they were pursued, jurisdictional lines forced city police to stop at the city line, and county police, at the county line. There were no effective state police, since only eleven states had them, and few of those were anything but traffic-enforcing agencies. It was not until Congress made federal crimes of most bank robberies, of crossing a state line after committing a felony, and of a number of other acts the bandits had been performing with impunity that effective action could be taken against them. Then in four years, from 1932 to

1936, the FBI wiped out the bank robbers virtually to the last man and last woman, mainly by killing them in gun battles.

When the bank-robber era ended in a hail of FBI bullets, it was gone forever. There are still bank robberies, of course, many by women, but usually they are quiet affairs in which the robber hands a teller a note and a paper sack, and walks out with that single sack filled with money. Occasionally there is an old-fashioned, spectacular one, such as the one Patty Hearst was convicted of participating in after her 1976 trial in San Francisco. But you no longer read of women such as Bonnie Parker, who roamed the country, hitting one bank after another, and shooting her way past road blocks. It just doesn't work anymore.

As long as the list of crimes described in this chapter is, it is still but a minute sampling of the crimes women have committed over the centuries. The main purpose in recounting them has been to show that though women have always committed fewer crimes than men, they are just as capable of committing every type of crime a man is capable of committing.

Chapter 4

The Literature of Female Criminality

In 1975 Dr. Freda Adler, associate professor of criminal justice at Rutgers University, published the results of a three-year study on the changing pattern of female crime in a book titled *Sisters in Crime*. It was the first and only in-depth study of the new criminality, and the only in-depth study of any facet of female criminality in recent years, other than one or two concerned solely with girl juvenile delinquents.

Researchers and scholars have never given female criminality the attention they gave male criminality. Most of what has been written on the subject has been included in books and reports on criminality in general, with the bulk of the data being devoted to male criminality, and whatever was included about women being appended as a sort of afterthought. There are probably two reasons for this. First, until relatively recently, the crime index for women has been too low to make it a significant social problem. Second, most of the researchers have been men.

There have been some scholarly writings concerned exclusively with female criminality, though. But almost without exception both the research upon which they were based and the conclusions drawn have been colored

by age-old myths about the nature of women in general—
that is, that women are passive, more emotional than men,
gentler in nature, and *inferior* to men.

The latter has been drilled into women for so many
centuries that the majority of them came to believe it.
Aristotle said, "Woman may be said to be an inferior
man." The Code of Manu, the Hindu book of law compiled somewhere around the first century, stipulated: "In
childhood a woman must be subject to her father; in youth
to her husband; when her husband is dead, to her sons. A
woman must never be free of subjugation." Lord Ches-
terfield, in a letter written to his son in 1748, counseled
him, "Women are to be talked to as below men, and above
children."

Such sentiments show clearly in the early writings on
female criminality, and more subtly even in many modern
writings. There has also been a tendency to divide all
women into two distinct classes: normal or "good"
women, and criminal or "bad" women, thus introducing
moral judgment into what was supposed to be scientific
research. Furthermore the approach of most researchers
has been to conclude in advance that female criminality
was the result of individual physical and psychological
traits. Economic and social conditions have been almost
totally ignored as causative factors, with the emphasis
being placed on such things as size (British researchers
John and Valerie Cowie and Eliot Slater found as recently
as 1968 in a study of delinquent girls that "bigness" may
lead to aggressiveness), early relationships with parents,
and even the menstrual cycle. (In a 1973 proposal for a
Center for the Study and Reduction of Violence at UCLA,
Dr. Louis J. West, director of the Neuropsychiatric Institute at that university, said that one of the studies would
involve the relationship between the menstrual cycle and
violence in women.)

Dr. Cesare Lombroso (1836–1909), an Italian psychiatrist, did the first important research of modern times into female criminality. His importance today is largely historical, since virtually all his conclusions have been discredited. His solution to female criminality was simply punishment, as he believed it incurable.

Since Lombroso, recommended methods of "undoing" female criminality have ranged all the way from psychoanalysis to lobotomy, but the common factor has been a belief that the individual criminal must be changed in some manner that will restore her to an acceptable role in society. Rehabilitative therapy is the commonest suggestion, a matter that will be touched on in some detail in the chapter on prisons. None of the writers suggests anything as radical as reforming our criminal-justice system, or instituting social programs designed to give the same opportunities to ghetto children that are available to children of the middle class.

Around the turn of the century Dr. Lombroso made an exhaustive study of the physical characteristics of female criminals. His data were obtained from the corpses and skeletons of harlots, pickpockets, murderesses, and other female criminals who had died in Italian jails.

The main fault with his once widely heralded study was that he set out with the advance notion that certain women were predestined from birth to become criminals, and that these latent criminals could be detected by their physical characteristics. That, as it happens, is the main fault of most subsequent studies of female criminality. It is difficult to understand why scholars and researchers in this field, with an occasional exception such as Adler, seem never to have heard of inductive reasoning, the standard method of laboratory scientists. Using inductive reasoning, the researcher gathers all available data, conducts all the experiments he can think of, then examines all the results to see what pattern emerges, *without having any preconceived notion of what that pattern might be.* Researchers into female criminality incline to use the deductive process, in which a basic premise is decided upon (such as Lombroso's belief that physical characteristics determine criminality), then data is reviewed in the light of either proving or disproving the premise. Given human nature, and the understandable reluctance of anyone to admit wasting perhaps years on a meaningless study, there is a natural tendency to find more data in support of a pet theory than against it.

That, unsurprisingly, is what happened in Lombroso's research. He found what he expected to find, that female criminals had certain physical traits lacking in normal women. These involved cranial size, the weight and width of the jawbone, the size and shape of cheekbones, the presence of moles, hairiness, and a variety of other physical characteristics. His conclusion was that women possessing a number of these physical traits could be identified as criminal types even before committing crimes, and thus society could take steps to protect itself against them. Since obviously the only workable "steps" would have been either to kill them or lock them up, his solution was meaningless. Even in nineteenth-century Italy people who had committed no crime couldn't be locked up simply because they had wide jawbones.

In *The Female Offender*, translated into English from the original Italian in 1903, Lombroso revealed a trait common to all early male writers on the subject, and even to a good many modern ones. He was insufferably paternalistic and condescending to women. In other words, he was what today's feminists would call a male chauvinist pig. In addition he was racist. He postulated a hierarchy of intelligence, in which the white man was supreme, and in which the nonwhite woman was at the bottom of the totem pole. He classed white women along with white children and all non-whites, all of which groups, he said, have fewer variations in their mental capacities than white men. He wrote:

> Even the female criminal is monotonous and uniform compared with her male companion, just as in general woman is inferior to man. . . .

He also wrote:

> Women have many traits in common with children; that their moral sense is deficient; that they are revengeful, jealous. . . In ordinary cases these defects are neutralized by piety, maternity, want of passion, sexual coldness, weakness and an undeveloped intelligence.

Thus, although women lacked the admirable traits of men, there were fewer female than male criminals because *normal* women also lacked the passion and intelligence to commit crimes, qualities which *criminal women* did not lack. Lombroso's experiments proved, at least to him, that the physical characteristics of criminal women were closer to those of both criminal and normal men than they were to those of normal women.

William Isaac Thomas (1863–1947) was a sociologist who taught at the University of Chicago for twenty-five years, but he did his most important work as an independent researcher after retirement. He wrote a number of books, but only two concerned female criminality. *Sex and Society* was published in 1907, *The Unadjusted Girl* in 1923. They are interesting for two reasons: Thomas moved on from Lombroso's explanation of female criminality in purely physical terms to include psychological and social causes (but without entirely abandoning physical reasons also), and he went through a change of thinking between publication of the two books.

Thomas, like Lombroso, took it for granted that women were inferior creatures. In commenting on their supposed (by him) ability to stand pain better than men, he wrote: "It is a logical fact . . . that the lower human races, the lower classes of society, women and children, show something of the same quality in their superior tolerance to surgical disease."

On the subject of female criminality Thomas lumped crime and morality together as equally important in maintaining social order. But he set different standards for men and women. Men were accountable for their actions to society at large, specifically to the male members of society, whereas women were primarily accountable to the men in their lives. Thomas made no bones about it being a male world, in which women were male property. He wrote:

> Morality, in the most general sense, represents the code under which activities are best carried on and is worked out in the school of experience. It is preeminently an adult and male system, and men are intelligent enough to realize that neither women nor children have passed through this school. It is on this account that man is merciless to woman from the standpoint of personal behavior, yet he exempts her from anything in the way of contractual morality, or views her defections in this regard with allowance and even with amusement.

By "contractual morality" he meant accountability to society at large. In other words, women could more easily get away with breaking laws than men, but they were forbidden to violate the male-set moral code.

Despite women's liberation and the new sexual freedom, there are remnants of this type of thinking even today. An example is that prostitutes are arrested, but not their male customers. However, this is beginning to change in some places, where local laws have recently been passed requiring the arrest of both.

The change in thinking Thomas underwent was that in his 1907 book he subscribed to the traditional belief that the solution to criminality was punishment. Sixteen years later, in *The Unadjusted Girl*, he had come to believe there were two better solutions—crime prevention and rehabilitation. In this work he refuted Lombroso's whole theory by denying that there was any such thing as a "crime-prone" person. He wrote:

> There is no individual energy, no unrest, no type of wish, which cannot be sublimated and made socially useful. From this standpoint, the problem is not the right of society to protect itself from the disorderly and antisocial person, but the right of the disorderly and antisocial person to be made orderly and socially valuable. . . . The problem of society is to produce the right attitudes in its members.

In simpler terms, the solution was to change the thinking of criminals and potential criminals so that they would docilely fit into the roles society preferred for them. This was a huge step toward modern thinking on the subject, but in other regards Thomas remained hopelessly Victorian in outlook. He was never able to distinguish between crime and sexuality, and to him "delinquent girls" were primarily those who were sexually promiscuous, as witness:

> The beginning of delinquency in girls is usually an impulse to get amusement, adventure, pretty clothes, favorable notice, distinction, freedom in the larger world. . . . The girls have usually become "wild" before the development of

sexual desire, and their casual sex relations do not usually awaken sex feeling. Their sex is used as a condition of the realization of other wishes. It is their capital.

The admonition here is pure Victorianism. Virtue is a commodity, which good girls save in order to trade for the eventual security of marriage. Bad girls expend this "capital" for temporary gains they are bound to regret eventually.

Thomas also seemed to be woefully ignorant of the economic conditions of his time. During a period when women worked sixteen hours a day in sweat shops, and people among the poorer classes actually sometimes starved to death, he was able to write:

> An unattached woman has a tendency to become an adventuress not so much on economic as on psychological grounds. Life is rarely so hard that a young woman cannot earn her bread; but she cannot always live and have the stimulation she craves.

Otto Pollak (1908——) is a professor of sociology at the University of Pennsylvania. His 1950 book, The Criminality of Women, has long been regarded as the definitive work on this subject to date. But again his conclusions are colored by the same time-worn myths about the nature of women that Lombroso and Thomas believed. Women are more sly and deceitful than men, more passive and more passionless. He was also influenced by the theories of Sigmund Freud, whose attitude toward women makes feminists climb walls.

Pollak added two new theories to the literature on female criminality.

The first was that women's crimes were primarily sexually motivated, whereas men's were primarily economically motivated, except for crimes of passion. In this he was reflecting the teachings of Freud, who believed that the basic problem of a neurotic and deviant woman was that she wished she were a man.

Freud coined the term "penis envy" to explain that little girls, when they first discovered they lacked something possessed by little boys, felt inferior and envious. According to Freud, women never got over this, although it eventually receded to the subconscious, so that they were unaware of their envy. Normal women attempted to compensate for their lack by making themselves as beautiful as possible, or by doing something men couldn't: have babies. Deviant women compensated by attempting to act like men, that is, commit crimes. The solution for both neurotic and deviant women, according to Freud, was to make them adjust to their proper (and inferior) sex role through psychoanalysis.

Since a whole generation accepted Freudian theories without a great deal of dissent, it is no reflection on Professor Pollak that he accepted this particular one.

The difficulty in criticizing Pollak is that to some extent he is right. Over the centuries women *have* committed different types of crimes from men, but whether this has been primarily because of different motivation or primarily because they have been thrust into different roles in life is a moot question. Prostitution may seem to be a sexually motivated crime, but there is at least as strong a case for its motivation being solely economic.

There may be truth in the suggestion that such female crimes as luring men into traps to be robbed are motivated at least partly by resentment against all men. However, Pollak tends to invent sexual motives for crimes committed by women when at best the evidence is slim. Women shoplifters are kleptomaniacs, for instance. Granted that shoplifting is a crime committed more by women than by men, there are male shoplifters. But you never hear of their being referred to as kleptomaniacs. Men caught in this crime are simply classed as petty thieves.

The second new theory Pollak advanced was that of "hidden" female crime, to account for what he considered a false low official crime rate for women. He believed that the type of crimes women commit are less likely to be detected, and therefore the difference between female and male crime indexes as officially reported did not represent the true difference.

One factor of this, according to Pollak, was the type of work women performed. Female domestics could steal from their employers with relative safety, whereas men had to commit burglary to steal the same items. Department-store clerks, mainly female, could steal merchandise with less chance of detection than nonemployees. Girls working in offices, nurses, and teachers had similar opportunities to steal with relatively little chance of being caught. Another factor was that women were naturally more stealthy than men, and more adept at concealing criminal acts.

A third factor was the chivalry of policemen and judges. Pollak wrote:

> One of the outstanding concomitants of the existing inequality . . . is chivalry, the general protective attitude of man toward woman. . . . Men hate to accuse women and thus indirectly send them to their punishment, police officers dislike to arrest them, district attorneys to prosecute them, judges and juries to find them guilty.

There may be validity in this, although some critics have pointed out that though such chivalry may be extended to upper-class and middle-class white women, it is less likely to be extended to lower-class and nonwhite women, and they make up the majority of those caught up in the criminal-justice system. As will be mentioned in a later chapter, there is evidence that this *has* been a factor regardless of female suspects' color or social class, but the new criminality among women seems to be changing the attitudes of both the police and the courts to handle women less and less differently from men. Pollak can hardly be faulted for that, though, since this development began to take place a quarter century after his book appeared.

One of the few women researchers into female criminality is Gisela Konopka, professor of social work at the University of Minnesota. Her research was confined to girl juvenile delinquents, and its results were published in 1966 in the book *Adolescent Girls in Conflict.*

Despite being a woman herself, Professor Konopka subscribed to many of the same old myths regarding the nature of women that earlier writers on the subject have advanced. She found a difference in the motives behind female and male crime very close to Pollak's theory. Referring to girl delinquents, she wrote: "Almost invariably her problems are deeply personalized. Whatever her offense—whether shoplifting, truancy or running away from home—it is usually accompanied by some disturbance or unfavorable behavior in the sexual area."

However, there is an important difference between the thinking of Pollak and that of Konopka. While Konopka believed there was a relationship between sex problems and delinquency, she didn't believe, like Pollak, that female crimes were sexually motivated. Her theory was that they sprang mainly from loneliness and dependency. At the same time delinquent girls were rebelling against authority, they were desperately in need of it. As she expressed it: "While these girls also strive for independence, their need for dependency is unusually great."

Like all theorists on the subject before her, Konopka took for granted that there were marked psychological differences between males and females. Girls were more concerned with their own personal feelings than boys, were more emotional, more dependent, and in greater need of social acceptance.

It is possible that all of these things are true, but there is growing doubt in psychological circles, particularly among psychologists with feminist leanings, that any of these differences are *inherent*. The feeling is that they are *conditioned* differences resulting from the societal roles thrust on women by a male-dominated society, in a kind of ongoing brainwashing process. If this is true, Konopka's solution to the problem of delinquency among girls falls apart, since her solution is therapy designed to adjust them to becoming good wives and mothers eventually. It is at least possible that the basic reason for the troubles of some delinquent girls is that they don't want to become good little wives and mothers.

A few other researchers deserve mention. Professor Sheldon Glueck (1896——) and Dr. Eleanor Glueck (1898——) are criminologists who spent years gathering data on hundreds of delinquent girls. In addition to tracing the girls' backgrounds and social histories, they compared their physical traits (much as Lombroso had compared the physical traits of dead criminals), and their psychological traits. The Gluecks' detailed report was published in 1934 under the title *Five Hundred Delinquent Women*. Their analysis was that female criminality results largely from biological and economic factors. They also found that an usually large percentage of these delinquent girls came from abnormally large families. This was hardly surprising, because a large percentage of delinquents has always come from poor families, and there are more large families among the poor than among any other group.

In 1967 one section of the *Report of the President's Commission on Law Enforcement and the Administration of Justice* was titled "The Female Offender." Walter Reckless and Barbara Kay, who prepared this part of the report, went back to Pollak's theory of hidden crime to explain the relatively low crime index for women. One part of their report reads:

> A large part of the infrequent officially acted upon involvement of women in crime can be traced to the masking effect of women's roles, effective practice on the part of women of deceit and indirection, their instigation of men to commit their crimes, and the unwillingness on the part of the public and law enforcement officials to hold women accountable for their deeds.

Dr. Clyde Vedder, professor of sociology and anthropology at Northern Illinois University, and Dora Somerville, commissioner of the Youth Commission for the State of Illinois, did a study of inmates in Illinois training schools for girls, the results of which were published as *The Delinquent Girl* in 1970. Dr. Vedder and Ms. Somerville explored various causes of juvenile delinquency ranging from psychological to social. Their work will be touched on in more detail in the section on girl delinquents.

Though there has been other research into female criminality, these accounts pretty well sum up the important research that has gone into the subject. Obviously it has been pretty scanty.

The main trouble with almost all studies to date is that they were based on too many ancient beliefs about the genetic nature of women. Most of these beliefs are rapidly becoming discredited by the latest thinking in the fields of psychology and anthropology. Dr. Freda Adler has managed to throw off the yoke of this traditional thinking in *Sisters in Crime*, but her study is confined primarily to the reasons for the increase and changing pattern of female crime in recent years. What is needed is an open-minded research program into all facets of female criminality by qualified persons uninhibited by traditional concepts that women are totally different from men psychologically, and are intellectually inferior to men.

Chapter 5

Causes of the Rise in Female Criminality

There is no simplistic explanation to what has brought about the tremendous increase of serious crimes by women in recent years. Numerous factors are involved. But one that gets a major share of the credit from some authorities is the women's liberation movement.

You can start fur flying in some quarters just by bringing up the subject. In October 1975 Los Angeles Police Chief Edward M. Davis, who frequently causes fur to fly with his controversial statements, aroused the ire of feminists by blaming not just the rise of female crime, but the increase of all crime at least partly on the women's liberation movement. The chief told a Los Angeles breakfast-club group that women in the movement do not stay home and give their children proper training. The breakdown in motherhood can lead to "the use of dope, stealing, thieving, and killing," Davis said. "If you don't have a culture in which to bring up a young human with love and discipline, he is going to become some type of human savage." The speech brought a spate of letters to the local papers, most denouncing his view, but a few, even from women, applauding it.

On the other side of the fence you can get equally

positive denials that the women's liberation movement has anything whatever to do with the increasing number of crimes by women. Kathy Rand, Midwest regional director of the National Organization for Women, commonly abbreviated as NOW, says, "Any connection in the rise of women arrested for major crimes and the women's liberation movement is incredible. There is nothing in the movement that encourages women to go out and commit crimes."

Ruth Glick, who conducted a federally funded study of women's correctional programs in the United States, not only denies that the women's liberation movement has had any effect on female criminality, but thinks the statistical evidence denoting a sharp increase in crime by women is misleading. At a March 1976 conference at Oakland, California, sponsored by the California Elected Women's Association, she told the delegates that though arrests by women may seem to have increased dramatically in recent years, the actual number of arrests is still small compared to that of men. Arrests of men still outnumber those of women by six to one, she said.

(She was quoting 1973 statistics. By 1974 the FBI *Uniform Crime Reports* showed the relationship as five to one, and showed an increase of serious crimes by women four and a half times greater than by men during that single year. The rate of increase slowed somewhat in 1975, but was still nearly double that of men. Serious crimes by men increased by 5.5 percent that year, while they jumped 9.4 percent for women. Thus the statistical evidence is not quite so misleading as she suggests.)

At the same conference Dr. Jennifer James, assistant professor of psychiatry at the University of Washington in Seattle, told the delegates, "The women behind bars are not feminists. They are women from classic female roles who are there because they have been accomplices to men, or have failed at the traditional roles of marriage and motherhood and turned to crime for economic reasons."

Dr. Freda Adler agrees with Dr. James that most women in jail are not feminists, but she disagrees that the women's liberation movement has had no influence on the rise in female criminality. Speaking of a female bank robber she interviewed in her study of more than fifteen hundred female offenders, Dr. Adler says in *Sisters in Crime*:

> Marge is a member of the new "liberation movement" which is spreading through the ranks of the nation's female offenders, but Marge would be the last person in the world to accredit her actions to any sort of "liberation." She, like the majority of incarcerated women throughout the country, comes from a lower socioeconomic level and tends to identify with a value code embracing the "traditional" image of women . . . Marge will not tolerate the mention of women's liberation. . . . She feels that "women's lib" is an organization of "kooks," and scoffs at the mention of any connection between her latest criminal actions and the beliefs of the female emancipation movement.

Nevertheless, Dr. Adler says, "Like her sisters in legitimate fields, the female criminal is fighting for her niche in the hierarchy."

The fact is that the women's liberation movement has opened up opportunities to *all* women, whether they consider themselves part of the movement or not, and even if they are philosophically opposed to it. There are now women fire fighters, women policemen walking beats and driving one-person squad cars instead of safely sitting behind desks, women truck drivers, telephone-line workers, deep-sea divers, preachers, and rabbis. Probably the majority do not consider themselves "women's libbers," and many may even feel much the same sort of scorn for the movement as bank robber Marge did. But they benefit from the new freedom the movement has brought about by taking full advantage of it. Sex roles are blurring more and more almost by the day. Women who even five years ago might have considered it "unfeminine" even to apply for jobs that have been traditionally male, now as a matter of course consider it their right to hold down any job they can handle.

It is hardly surprising that female criminals have a similar attitude. The same women in prison who express scorn for the feminist movement are likely to bridle with resentment if asked why they strayed from "traditional" female crimes, such as shoplifting, to male crimes, such as bank robbery. Dr. Adler cites one inmate of a New York women's prison, in for robbery, who was offended at being asked if she had been arrested for shoplifting. "You wouldn't catch me doing no boosting," the woman said, implying that such "small stuff" was beneath her dignity.

Why some feminists are so disturbed by the suggestion that the women's liberation movement has anything to do with the rise in female crime is hard to understand. It is no criticism of the movement to surmise that *all* women are being released from the chains that bound them to accepted traditional roles, including female criminals. And it is mere rationalization to protest that few women criminals are also feminists. Large numbers of women who have moved into "male" jobs do not believe in the movement. Since feminists are not in the least reluctant to credit the movement for these women's gains, it is somewhat illogical to insist that the new freedom of opportunity does not apply to the one particular group classed as women criminals.

In addition to changing traditional attitudes about what

is acceptable behavior for women, the women's liberation movement has opened up opportunities previously unavailable to female criminals. One of the reasons the three traditional female crimes for so many years remained shoplifting, bad-check passing, and prostitution is that the majority of women were limited to those choices by their roles in life. It was impossible for a housewife to become an embezzler, simply because she had no access to company funds. She had excellent opportunity to shoplift, however, because she did most of the family shopping. For the same reason she was in a position to cash bad checks. And prostitution was the easiest criminal activity of all for any woman, married or not, to get into, because it required no training, no experience, and there was no male competition.

Greater opportunity to commit so-called white collar crimes is reflected in the increase of frauds by women during the period from 1960 to 1975. While there was an increase of only 91.1 percent in male arrests for these crimes, women's arrests jumped by a whopping 488.5 percent. In 1960 nearly six times as many men as women were arrested for fraud (29,695 as opposed to 5,111); in 1975 the ratio had dropped to less than twice as many male as female arrests (56,736 to 30,076).

Dr. Lawrence Z. Freedman, professor of psychiatry at the University of Chicago, who specializes in the study of antisocial behavior, predicts that this trend will continue, with more and more women committing crimes previously committed only by men in high executive positions in business and industry, such as price-fixing, embezzling, and violations of the antitrust laws.

He says, "As women move into financial and corporate management positions, they will have the same opportunities as men to commit these kinds of financial crimes, and there is no reason to believe they will be any more or less susceptible to the opportunities than are men."

Dr. Freedman's comment reflects the consensus among modern-day psychologists and psychiatrists, who find no evidence that women are either any more honest or dishonest than men. It is therefore hardly surprising that the rate of embezzlement by women is rising in proportion to the number of women moving into jobs involving custody of funds. Similarly violations of public trust by women have increased simply because there are more women in positions to accept bribes, and the number is growing as more and more women become law-enforcement officers, judges, and are elected to public office.

To some extent even the increase in crimes such as robbery, burglary, and car theft by women can be attributed to increased opportunity. Professor Gene Kassebaum of the University of Hawaii, in referring to women's status before the women's liberation movement, comments, "Just as there were more job opportunities open to men, even where women were equally qualified, it was also true for criminal opportunities. A perfectly well-qualified girl was discriminated against if she wanted to be a car thief. No one taught her how."

Now such well-qualified girls have demanded training from the male car thieves in their peer groups, though, and have passed it on to their girl friends. During the decade between 1960 and 1970 motor-vehicle thefts by women doubled. In the period from 1960 to 1975 they increased by 163.2 percent, whereas motor-vehicle thefts by males went up only 35.6 percent. Male auto thefts actually dropped by 5.3 percent between 1974 and 1975, while those by females rose by 0.8 percent.

Probably as important a factor in the rising female crime rate as either the new freedom or wider opportunities is the changed attitude in the underworld of crime as to what is acceptable behavior by women criminals. The attitudes of both sexes seem to have undergone radical change. Traditionally women criminals with male partners have been in subservient roles. The typical gun moll acted as a lookout, a caser of jobs, a holder of loot until the heat died down, and as a sex partner. Quite often she was also a punching bag to release her man's frustrations, and was expected to accept her black eyes stoically as one of her functions. While many female criminals still remain in somewhat subservient roles, large numbers have rebelled.

An investigative reporter for the *Los Angeles Times* recently interviewed a dozen prostitutes working the vicinity of Hollywood and Vine in Hollywood. Traditionally prostitutes have attached themselves to male parasites known as pimps, who took most of the money they earned. Of the twelve interviewees, only one admitted supporting a pimp, and she was considering discarding him. The other eleven were emphatic in their rejection of the idea. The general feeling was expressed by a twenty-two-year-old black girl who said, "I ran that road a couple of years, but no more. No man's going to do me ever again. Who needs them?"

Indications from other parts of the country also are that pimping as a profession is coming to an end. A similar check, by a news team, of prostitutes working the Times Square district of Manhattan disclosed that most were independents. An even more surprising discovery was that some were middle-class housewives, free-lancing in order to pick up extra household money.

Since prostitutes have always been the most male-dominated class of female criminals (by their pimps and procurers), the phenomenon of large numbers of them throwing off the yoke of male domination is in the nature of a revolution. It is therefore hardly surprising that other female criminals are exhibiting similar independence. While male-female bank-robber teams go clear back to the 1930's, the lone female bandit, or team of female bandits, is a brand-new development.

The plight of even those female criminals who remain male-dominated seems to be changing. Roy Gerard, assistant director for correctional programs at the U.S. Bureau of Prisons, says: "Women used to be outside during a bank robbery as lookouts or to drive the getaway car. Now they are inside with the guns robbing the bank."

Though part of the reason gun molls have moved inside the banks may be simply because they have demanded more equal treatment from their men, probably a larger reason is that their male partners no longer consider such actions outside women's roles. A changed attitude similar to that displayed toward the molls of the bank-robber era of the 1930's seems to have developed among today's male criminals.

There is tremendous social pressure at all socio-economic levels to conform to certain standards of behavior. An ancient gypsy proverb says, "The white crow is pecked from the nest." Human beings punish others in their peer group who dare to be "different" by ostracizing them. It is not likely that a gun moll would assist her man in a bank robbery with a gun if such aggressive action were not generally accepted as permissible within her peer group—no more so than it would be likely for Jacqueline Onassis to chew tobacco in public.

In 1973 anthropologist Walter B. Miller of the Center for Criminal Justice at Harvard Law School reported on a two-and-a-half-year study of an all-girl juvenile gang called the Molls in an east-coast city. Social workers kept in constant contact with the girls during the two and a half years. The Molls' membership underwent some changes during the period of the study, but they averaged about eleven members, mostly from laboring-class Irish Catholic families. The study disclosed that one motivation for the girls' delinquent behavior was desire to win approval from an all-male juvenile gang called the Hoods.

The girls ranged in age from about thirteen and a half to sixteen. Offenses for which they were arrested during the period of study included theft, drinking violations, and vandalism, as well as assault in connection with fights with another all-girl gang. The research team found that though the Molls themselves recognized that their delinquent actions stemmed from several motives, they were aware that an important one was to gain acceptance and approval from the Hoods, and they felt the way to do that was to emulate the boys' behavior.

Ten years earlier such behavior by girls in that same neighborhood would have been unthinkable, because the Hoods' girls were expected to act only as subservient assistants in the boys' activities. As a matter of fact, even the formation of an all-girl gang would have been unthinkable. Girl gang members merely belonged to the auxiliaries of boys' gangs, where they functioned in the traditional roles of lookouts, spies, errand girls, and sex partners. Though they often carried weapons for the boys before "rumbles," so that the boys would be "clean" if stopped by police en route to battle, the girls disappeared when the fighting started. But now they carry their own weapons, and use them. And the boys approve.

Since the attitudes of juvenile gangs in ghetto areas tend to reflect the attitudes of former members, often admired by the youngsters, who have graduated to adult criminality, acceptance of the new aggressiveness among

juvenile girls by juvenile boys is at least a strong indication of a similar change in thinking in the adult underworld.

The increased use of narcotics is accepted by virtually
all authorities as a major cause of the general increase in
crime. Opinions as to how responsible drugs are for the
increase in serious crimes by women vary, though.

Kenneth Bishop, superintendent of the Massachusetts
Correctional Institution at Farmingham, estimates that 15
to 20 percent of the female prisoners are there for drug
possession or sale, or for crimes committed to support a
habit. Kenneth McDannell, warden of the Morgantown
Federal Prison in West Virginia, says, "At least sixty percent of the prisoners here are in for narcotics, or some
drug-related crime such as bank robbery or armed robbery. It's the drugs, not the Women's Lib thing."

In direct opposition to such opinions, spokesmen for
the subculture, where drugs are most used, notably Dr.
Timothy Leary, scoff at the notion that there is any significant relationship between drug use and crime. They
point out that marijuana is so commonly used that some
researchers estimate that half the adult population of the
United States has at least tried it, and that cocaine, which is
not addictive, has become a fad among the rich. Where
narcotics have swelled the crime rate is largely in arrests
for possession and sale, the argument goes—both victimless crimes that shouldn't even be on the books. Virtually
all law authorities reject the notion that sale of narcotics is
a victimless crime, although many agree that mere possession is.

In order to put the argument in perspective, one hard
fact should be looked at that both sides tend to ignore,
namely that narcotic-drug-law offenses are Part II crimes
in the *Uniform Crime Reports*, and therefore have no effect on the statistics for serious crimes.

Both sides present some specious arguments.

One of the commonest from the pro-drug faction is that drugs are neither more physically harmful nor more crime-inducing than alcohol. Insofar as marijuana is concerned, more and more medical authorities are coming to agree that it is less harmful than alcohol. But hard drugs, such as heroin, are another thing. It is probably true that as many people die of acute alcoholism as of drug overdoses, and it is undoubtedly true that many crimes have been committed under the influence of alcohol that might not have been committed if the perpetrators had been sober. But you never hear of a teenager holding up a gas station in order to support an alcohol habit. Even a chronic drunk would find it hard to spend more than perhaps $50 a week on booze, if he bought it by the bottle instead of by the drink in expensive bars. But heroin addicts have been known to develop habits costing several hundred dollars a week. Since most such addicts are young, uneducated, and frequently unemployed, the only way they can possibly raise that much is by committing crimes. To suggest that increased drug use has not been a direct cause of many crimes being committed is ridiculous.

The antidrug faction tends to exaggerate in the other direction. There is no question that illegal drugs have become a national problem. In 1960 there were only 25,857 arrests for narcotic-drug-law violations in the whole country. In 1975 there were 291,061, an increase of 1,025.7 percent. However, only a minute portion of these arrests were of big-time dealers such as the one in the movie The French Connection. The FBI defines this category as "Offenses relating to narcotic drugs, such as unlawful possession, sale, use, growing, manufacturing, and making of narcotic drugs." There is no statistical breakdown to show how many arrests involved hard drugs as compared to soft drugs, such as marijuana; how many were dealers; and how many were simply possessors and users. All narcotics arrests are lumped together. A random check of police blotters around the country indicates that probably the majority were for simple possession of marijuana, amphetamines (pep pills), and barbiturates (downers), which drastically alters the picture the bald statistics give of a nation of dope fiends.

Insofar as the use of drugs by women is concerned, the percentage increase since 1960 has been about the same as for men. The male increase has been 1,028 percent, the female increase 1,011.9 percent. In actual arrests, 22,124 males were booked in 1960, 249,552 in 1975. Female arrests for the same period rose from 3,733 to 41,509. If the number of arrests bears any relationship to the number of users, it would seem that only about one sixth of the drug users in the country are women.

The specter of every drug addict robbing banks to support an insatiable habit is largely fantasy, particularly insofar as female addicts are concerned. They have a means of illegal income to support their habits which is unavailable to men. There is little question that narcotic addiction drives many women into prostitution, but for every female addict who takes that road to raise money to support her habit, there is one less potential female bank robber.

All factors considered, it would seem that though narcotics use undoubtedly has created some female criminals, it is not an important cause of the increase in serious crimes by women.

One reason for the general increase in crime, both by men and women, is simply population growth, as it is only logical to expect a greater number of criminals among a greater number of people. To adjust for this automatic factor, the *Uniform Crime Reports*, in one of its tables, computes the percentage increase in the different categories of crime by each 100,000 of population. Unfortunately the figures are not broken down into arrests by sex.

Violent crimes committed by both sexes increased by 255.8 percent from 1960 to 1975, but when computed on the basis of increase per-capita, the figure is only 199.3 percent. For crimes against property, the real increase was 230.5 percent, the per capita increase 178.1 percent. The total increase in all or serious (Part I) crimes was 233 percent; figured on a per-capita basis it was 180 percent.

Thus when the population growth is taken into consideration, the percentage increase in serious crimes by both sexes is reduced by a little over one fourth. But the figure of a general increase in serious crimes of 180 percent over a fifteen year period is still pretty alarming. It would take a computer to figure out just how the percentages given for female crimes should be adjusted to take into account population growth, but even if they are all reduced by 25 percent, they remain just as alarming.

The factor of chivalry has already been mentioned in Chapter 4 as part of Pollak's theory of "hidden crime." An increasingly less chivalrous attitude on the parts of the police and the courts is thought by some authorities to be a factor in the rising rate of female crime. The theory is that more women are being arrested simply because fewer are being let off with admonishments by male arresting officers who traditionally have been reluctant to arrest women if they could avoid it.

Professor of Criminology Robert Coggins, whose classes at Central Piedmont Community College in Charlotte, North Carolina, contain many policemen, says: "Some police officers say that female crime really isn't increasing that much, but that the police are getting more diligent in arresting females. Men had been taught that the female was someone to be reserved for a special place. They just hated taking a woman to a police station and locking her up in an old cell."

An exactly opposite opinion is expressed by Howard Garrigan, chief of the Detention and Corrections Division of the Alameda County Sheriff's Office in California, who says: "The female crime trend is something the criminal justice system hasn't caught up with. The woman in crime will still get breaks that would not be allowed for a man."

Agreeing with this point of view, a spokesman for the California State Department of Corrections was quoted in the March 1976 issue of *The Law Enforcement Journal* as having said: "The chances of a woman going to prison are a lot less than a man's. This is partly because of male chauvinism, the reluctance to separate women from children, and the feeling that women are not as much of a threat as men. A woman is more likely to get probation or a short county-jail sentence than to wind up in a state prison."

The fact seems to be that traditionally both chivalry and male paternalism have been factors in the treatment of female criminals not only by the police, but by the courts and by prison authorities. This will be explored in more detail, and will be supported by some evidence other than personal opinions, in later chapters. It suffices here to say that it seems to have been a mixed blessing for female criminals. The tendency has been to treat women accused of minor crimes more leniently than men accused of the same crimes, but to treat them more harshly than men for serious crimes. If there is a general change taking place in the way women are being treated in the criminal-justice system, there is no data other than some scattered personal opinions to support the guess that it is having an effect on the number of women arrested.

Other factors have been suggested as contributing to the general increase in crime, such as a growing amount of emotional imbalance due to the increasing pace of every-day living in a progressively more technologized society, the rise in unemployment, parental permissiveness, and a general breakdown in morality. But in this book we are not so much concerned with the general increase in crime. Our concern is primarily with the increase in female crim-inality, and though all these factors may have contributed to the general increase, they offer no explanation for the fact that female criminality is increasing at a much more rapid rate than male criminality.

Nothing in any of the four above-mentioned factors, for instance, explains why from 1973 to 1974 serious crimes by women jumped four and a half times as much as seri-ous crimes by men, then jumped twice as much as men's crimes in 1975. Nor does population growth, or the in-creased use of narcotics account for it.

In reviewing works in their field, sociologists tend to be rather intolerant of conclusions drawn which are not based on "hard data." For example, in a review by a fellow sociologist of Pollak's *The Criminality of Women*, which appeared in *Issues in Criminology*, a social-science jour-nal in criminology and corrections, these statements ap-pear: (1) "These conjectures seem hardly supported by the references Pollak uses." (2) "No data is provided in sup-port of such a conclusion." (3) ". . . a contention not supported by the data." (4) ". . . even the table used by Pollak does not fully support his thesis."

Sociology is not an exact science, however, and hard data are sometimes very difficult to come by. There is really no way to measure what percentage each possible cause has contributed to the rise in female criminality. In order to come to any conclusions at all, it is necessary to make some educated guesses.

I am therefore going to stick my neck out by expressing an opinion that I freely admit is based more on an overall impression I got from researching this book than on any measurable data. That impression is that the greatest single causative factor in the increase of female criminality has been the women's liberation movement.

The effect has been entirely indirect, I believe. Kathy Rand of NOW was quite correct when she said, "There is nothing in the movement that encourages women to go out and commit crimes." But the movement has opened opportunities to all women that were formerly barred to them. It has caused them to reevaluate their status in relation to men, and in many cases to come to the defiant conclusion expressed by Ethel Merman in the musical comedy *Annie Get Your Gun* when she sang, "Anything you can do, I can do better." And it has changed the attitude of society in general, including the male segment of it, as to what is acceptable behavior for women.

The fact that these social changes, beneficial to all women, have also been causative factors in the increase of female criminality, is in no way a reflection on the movement. If all women are eventually to obtain full equality with men, it must be accepted that female criminals cannot be excluded. When the time is reached that police forces are composed of an equal number of men and women, we may anticipate that there probably will also be just as many female bank robbers as male ones.

Chapter 6

The Women's Liberation Movement

It is my personal belief that the women's liberation movement is such an important factor in the rising rate of female criminality that it merits a detailed look at what it is all about.

Sigmund Freud said, "The great question that has never been answered, and which I have not yet been able to answer despite my thirty years of research into the feminine soul, is: What does a woman want?" We might paraphrase that by asking: "What does a women's libber want?"

She claims she simply wants freedom from the yoke of male oppression under which she has suffered since Adam and Eve were evicted from the Garden of Eden. She says she wants both economic and social equality with men. She denies that the physical differences between the sexes, which have been the root cause of the discrimination against her, are as important as men have always insisted.

There are marked physical differences between the sexes, of course. In addition to the primary sex differences, such as reproductive organs and women's breasts, there are a number of what biologists call secondary sex characteristics. Men have heavier bone structures and are more heavily muscled. Women average about two thirds the strength of men and have broader pelvises. Women tend to be more dexterous with their fingers than men, can stand both higher and lower temperatures, and can hear higher sound waves than men.

Obviously men and women were not created physically equal. But when opponents of the movement advance this as an argument against it, the feminists' response to these critics is that they simply don't understand what the movement is all about. With a few radical exceptions—and every social movement, including all the great religious movements, has had a lunatic fringe—feminists say they have no interest in equal opportunity to become linebackers for the Pittsburgh Steelers. They are simply demanding an end to economic discrimination in areas where they are capable of competing with men, and an end to the social discrimination stemming from male-set rules that narrowly prescribe acceptable behavior for women, but which condone virtually any noncriminal behavior by men.

The concept that men have a natural right to dominate women because they are larger and stronger may have been valid when both lived in caves, but power in our modern technological society has nothing to do either with size or with physical strength. Some of the most powerful men in the world are physically smaller than the average woman. Henry Kissinger is shorter than his wife. Neither Henry Ford nor John D. Rockefeller were muscular men, yet the displeasure of either could make larger men quail. For many years the late Howard Hughes was an ailing recluse, yet he ruled one of the world's financial empires. There are no physical characteristics that would have made a woman any less effective in any of these roles.

The average feminist makes no attempt to claim physical equality with men. Her claim is that physical differences are not a valid reason for the discriminatory treatment afforded her. More important than the physical differences between the two sexes, she says, is their psychological similarities. Though traditionally there has been little such similarity, she claims this is due to conditioning and that there are no inherent differences. Her argument is that men and women develop differently mainly because of an insidious shaping process that begins virtually at birth.

Both girls and boys submit to this shaping process by doing what is expected of them largely because it is virtually impossible for the average person to go against what psychologists call "role expectations." Pressures on little boys to be "manly" and on little girls to be "feminine" come from their parents, their peers, and from society at large with irresistible force.

Boys are expected to climb trees, to run and shout, and to attract dirt. Parents complain with proud despair that Junior can't keep the knees in his Levi's. Boys are given footballs, baseballs, aggression-teaching toys such as boxing gloves, cap pistols, and BB guns, and achievement-developing toys such as erector sets and model-airplane kits. Girls are expected to play quietly, to stay clean, and to be so easy on clothing that they never outwear it, but only outgrow it. They are given soft, cuddly toys, or toys requiring little physical activity, such as tea sets and doll dishes. Their toys usually require less skill to use than the toys given boys, and when skills are required, they are usually in narrowly designated areas. Sewing and baking kits are all right, and even nursing kits, but not toy trucks or electric trains.

Little boys must never cry, whereas not only little girls, but even grown women are permitted tears, and often

learn to use them as a device to get their way with the
men in their lives. In our culture a little boy may give his
mother an occasional hug, but such an expression of affection to his father would at best be accepted awkwardly. A
little girl, on the other hand, may distribute her affection
indiscriminately, and is merely thought "sweet" for it.

Nonconformity is less tolerated in boys than in girls.
"Sissies" generally get bad treatment from their peers.
Tomboys are regarded with more indulgence, but only
when their tomboyishness is considered a temporary
phase. They are expected to grow out of it, and usually do.
Jerome Kagan and H. A. Moss in their 1962 book *Birth to
Maturity* reported on a research study that found both
sissies and tomboys reverse themselves as they mature,
with dependent boys generally developing into aggressive men, and aggressive girls becoming typically dependent women. This seems to indicate that in the majority of
cases society succeeds in enforcing role expectations in
the long run, even among rebel children.

The desire to conform is a tremendous social pressure.
Despite the tradition of rugged individualism in America,
very few people want to be considered markedly different
from what is accepted as "normal." Men who act "effemi-
nate" are regarded either with derision or disdain, as are
"masculine" women. Most of us like to be regarded as
"different" in its complimentary meaning of being somehow superior to the norm, but we have no desire to be
thought so different as to be regarded as freakish. There is
considerable revelation of human nature in the wistful
words of the teenager at the height of the hippie movement, who said, "I want to be a nonconformist, like every-
body else."

Feminists can present considerable historical evidence
to document their charge of systematic oppression by

men. In virtually all ancient societies women were regarded as male property, and they still are in a few present-day societies. In primitive tribes brides often are bought, thus becoming their husbands' personal property by right of purchase. In all the great religions women are accorded lower status than men. The Tenth Commandment, which is law to both Jews and Christians, reads: "Thou shalt not covet thy neighbour's house, thou shalt not covet thy neighbour's wife, nor his manservant, nor his maidservant, nor his ox, nor his ass, nor any thing that is thy neighbour's." In ancient Israel all these items were male property. The manservant and maidservant were property because they were slaves. It is indicative of the wife's status under Old Testament law that she was lumped together with slaves, livestock, and real estate as an equally valuable asset.

The Koran, the sacred book of the Muslims, similarly designates women as property. Thus Judaism, Christianity, and Islam, all worshipping the same God under different names and constituting about 37 percent of the world's population, give religious sanction to the inferiority of women. The other five great religions in terms of membership—Confucianism, Buddhism, Hinduism, Shintoism, and Taoism—all give men the bulk of legal rights, although some of them grant women certain ritualistic rights, such as deference from sons. About 26 percent of the world's population are believers in one of these five. Since among them the eight religions with the largest numbers of followers comprise 63 percent of the world's population, it is evident that their teachings have been a major force in establishing the historical role of woman in society.

There have been some matriarchal societies, but even in them women didn't really run things. Modern anthropologists have come to the nearly unanimous conclusion that primitive societies dominated by women are wholly mythical. The legendary Amazons never really existed except in storytellers' imaginations. All that most so-called matriarchates amounted to was that descent was traced through the female line and a mother's children belonged to her clan instead of to their father's. There is no evidence that women held ruling authority in any society, ever. Their dominance, if any, was largely ritualistic. In ancient China, for instance, even a grown son was expected to prostrate himself before his mother and beg forgiveness if he had offended her, yet she had no property rights and might be totally dependent on the son for her support.

Polygamy, common in many ancient societies and still practiced in some Eastern and Near Eastern cultures, is considered by feminists as the ultimate in female subjugation. As it happens, polyandry—the custom of women having more than one husband at the same time—has been rather widespread too. But the two are hardly comparable. In ancient times polygamy often involved harems, in which women were penned like cattle, cut off from all associations other than the other wives and children in the harem except on the occasions the husband deigned to see them. There was never any comparable degradation of men under polyandry, nor did the practice develop in any advanced societies. Though it has not been confined solely to primitive tribes, it has been confined to societies where there is a low level of technological development, such as the Todas of southern India, the Gilyaks of Siberia, and a group of Tibetans in the Himalayan Mountains. Primitive tribes practicing the custom include some in Africa and South America, in Alaska, in the Canary Islands, Madagascar, the Malay Archipelago, and on some South Sea islands.

Anthropologists have discovered that in all cases polyandry, like polygamy, was a male idea, usually instituted to free the man from the burden of having to support a wife and family by himself, and was not caused by any shortage of women. The *Encyclopedia Americana* says: "The emphasis in polyandry is on men choosing to share a wife, and not on a woman deciding to have two or more husbands." In any event, wherever polyandry has been practiced, it has been merely a permitted custom, not a general one. Most marriages are monogamous, and the bride has no say in the decision of whether or not to add additional husbands to the family. Thus in polyandrous societies women are actually as subject to male rule as in polygamous societies.

The concept of chivalry, which flowered during the Middle Ages and persists to some extent even today, improved the lot of women in some ways, but it simultaneously added new chains. It raised women from their traditional inferiority to a position of superiority to men. But it was only a spiritual superiority. They moved from the harem to a pedestal, where they stood with hands demurely folded as semigoddesses—adored, revered, respected, protected, and pampered. But this new reverence had to be earned by living up to a rigid code of behavior prescribed by men. And there was no forgiveness for straying from the prescribed code. Women were either chaste or fallen, and the fallen were outcasts, scorned not only by men, but also by their own sisters.

Modesty was nearly as rigid a requirement as chastity. A nineteenth-century novel, considered risqué at the time, owed its phenomenal success to the importance attached to feminine modesty. The heroine of the novel was a young woman whose father faced financial ruin because of the machinations of an unscrupulous businessman. She sought out the businessman at the hotel where he stayed to plead with him to show her father mercy. He agreed to release her father from all financial obligations, on condition that she let him see her naked. He promised not to touch her, but only to look. She accepted, but insisted that he perform his part of the bargain first. To ensure that he wouldn't be cheated out of his reward, the businessman required her to swear on the Bible that she would go through with it after he had saved her father. In due course the necessary signed releases were delivered to the father, and the villain demanded his reward. The girl agreed to meet him for dinner at his hotel to discuss when and where she would pay off. At the appointed hour she walked into the crowded hotel dining room, wearing a long coat, and approached his table. As he rose to his feet to greet her, she slipped off the coat, under which she wore nothing, stood before him (and the other shocked diners) nude for a moment, then fell down dead. She had taken a slow poison designed to kill her at that precise moment.

This act of feminine idiocy caused so many readers to weep in sympathy that the novel became a best seller.

While this highly dramatic plot could only cause present-day readers to roll in the aisles, the double standard has far from disappeared. As will be shown in the section on delinquency in girls, society still condemns sexual activity by girls while tacitly condoning it by boys. As for adult women, the new sexual freedom so far seems to be confined to the more liberal elements of our society, and to have hardly affected traditional middle-class attitudes. If you doubt that, bring up the subject at a PTA meeting. America's middle-class majority seems to equate the new morality with moral decay, and to yearn for a return to the old values.

Although we have come a long way toward equality for

women, there is still another long way to go, according to feminists. They claim there is considerable myth about just how much freedom they have gained. There is, for instance, the often-repeated statement that women control the money in this country. The fact that the majority of bank accounts, stocks, bonds, and similar holdings are either jointly owned by husbands and wives or are in the names of women does not mean women control the wealth. In most cases, feminists charge, such holdings are arranged by males strictly for their own convenience, or their own financial benefit. It is common practice for housewives to have checking accounts in their names, for instance, but this is simply to relieve the husband of the chore of handling household expenses, and expenditures are often closely supervised by the husband. Savings and securities are often placed in wives' names for tax reasons, to protect the husbands from having to pay judgments, or to avoid inheritance taxes. The women have little actual control of this wealth, however, in that few of them sit on boards of directors, and if their votes as stockholders are required, usually they simply hand their husbands their proxies.

The suggestion that women really run things in this country by indirection also irritates feminists. The theory here is that through cajolery, tears, and other feminine wiles, women easily get their way with men. It is probably true that many a fur coat has been obtained that way, but the concept that such devices have a noticeable effect on political or economic decisions at a high level seems very questionable. And even where such devices are effective, feminists consider it degrading to have to use them. They point out that only those in an inferior position would have to use such tactics to get what they want, and that the so-called feminine techniques are remarkably similar to the ones formerly used by Negro slaves to wheedle favors from their masters.

"The hand that rocks the cradle rules the world" is a nice ringing phrase, but feminists doubt that it even rules the household.

Although the women's liberation movement has begun to gain appreciable success only in recent years, it is by no means a new movement. There has been a steady procession of activist women fighting for it since the middle of the nineteenth century. A representative sample of the better-known ones would have to include this dozen:

Fanny Wright (1795–1852) was America's first woman lecturer. She fought for both women's and workingmen's rights, opposed debtor's prison, proposed public schools, and shocked the nation by advocating birth control.

Emma Willard (1787–1870) was an educator who fought for women to get the same educational advantages as men.

Lucretia Mott (1793–1880), another advocate of women's rights, was one of the first American women to demand the abolition of slavery.

Amelia Bloomer (1818–1894) advocated a number of social reforms, including women's rights, but is best remembered for the item of female apparel she promoted—bloomers.

Harriet Beecher Stowe (1811–1896) is best known as the author of *Uncle Tom's Cabin*, the novel that inflamed the North against slavery, and that caused Abraham Lincoln to comment upon meeting her shortly after the start of the Civil War, "So you are the little woman who brought on this great conflict." But she was also a vigorous and vocal women's rights advocate.

Frances Elizabeth Willard (1839–1898) was an educator and lecturer who, according to her biographers, worked for thirty-nine different reforms during her lifetime, including temperance, better schools, clean politics, curbs on lobbying, labor reform, prison reform, police matrons, peace, nutrition, kindergarten, and women's rights.

Elizabeth Cady Stanton (1815–1902) campaigned for women's suffrage, for property rights for women, and for women's rights to divorce their husbands on the grounds of drunkenness or brutality.

Susan B. Anthony (1820–1906) is probably the best known of all women's suffrage workers, and is the one person historians usually credit as most responsible for the passage of the Fourteenth Amendment, popularly known as the Reconstruction Amendment, giving equal protection under the law to all citizens of the United States.

Carry Nation (1846–1911) is primarily remembered as the violent temperance fanatic who went around the country breaking up saloons with an ax, but she was also a strong advocate of women's suffrage.

Belva Ann Lockwood (1830–1917), America's first woman lawyer, twice ran for President, in 1884 and 1888, on the National Equal Rights Party ticket. She polled few votes, largely because only men were able to vote. She died three years before the Nineteenth Amendment gave the vote to women.

Emmeline Pankhurst (1858–1928) was English instead of American, but a list of women's rights leaders would hardly be complete without her. In 1903 she founded the Women's Social and Political Union, an organization that attracted worldwide attention because of its militant fight for suffrage. Instead of just lecturing, members picketed, marched, and demonstrated, often bringing about confrontations with the police. Repeatedly jailed for offenses ranging from refusing to obey police orders to disperse to inciting riot, she was the first person ever to use the hunger strike as a means of protest.

Jane Addams (1860–1935) was a social worker who founded Hull House of Chicago, a welfare agency committed to helping the needy, providing recreational facilities for juveniles, and a number of other social causes. President of the International Women's Congress at the Hague in 1915 and a delegate to subsequent Congresses in other cities around the world, she was also an active woman suffragist, and the only one of the above list who lived to see the day that she could exercise her vote in the United States.

There was a long moratorium on women's-rights activism after the Nineteenth Amendment went into effect in 1920. Simultaneously with women's right to vote, many of the traditional social restrictions on women were scrapped as the country moved from the prudish Victorian era into the roaring twenties. Freed of their long hair, whalebone corsets, and ankle-length dresses, women were as welcome in the new speakeasies as men, and while the pre-World-War-I saloons had been strictly male clubs, most women were under the impression that they *had* obtained freedom. Women activists generally turned to other causes, such as temperance, child-labor laws, and similar reforms. A few scattered voices protested that the fight was far from over, but in general the feeling that it had been won persisted among the majority of women right through the twenties and thirties, up until World War II.

World War II gave a push to women's liberation that went largely unrecognized at the time. With a goodly proportion of the male labor force having been drafted into the armed forces, the nation turned to women to fill the gap. Amid considerable patriotic drum beating women were urged to "do their parts" by helping build tanks, airplanes, and guns. In torrents housewives who had never worked outside the home flocked to the factories to work on assembly lines, run lathes and drill presses, to operate welding and burning torches, grinding machines, and to run cranes. "Rosie the Riveter" became a national symbol representing the American woman's contribution to the war effort.

A phenomenon that went unnoticed outside law-enforcement circles during this period was that women's crimes, according to FBI statistics, increased nearly 100 percent from 1940 to 1945, then decreased again after the end of the war. Various explanations have been offered for this. One that sounds logical is that uncaught male criminals were being drafted into the armed forces along with the other draftees, and women began moving into the vacancies left in the ranks of the underworld, just as their legitimate sisters were moving into vacancies left in industry by the draft. Another explanation is that crime always goes up in wartime because of a general relaxation of moral values, combined with a widespread feeling that nothing matters much because there may be no tomorrow. Since a large proportion of the men who ordinarily would have been committing crimes were in service, this natural increase was reflected mainly in crimes by women. Whatever the reason, crimes by women began decreasing as soon as the boys started to return from overseas.

It had been taken for granted by government and industry alike, when the call went out for women to "do their parts" in the war effort, that once the emergency was over they would return to their "natural" roles as housewives and mothers. Many did, but also many didn't. Having crossed the sex barrier into jobs previously barred to them by male rules, these dissidents had no desire to return to the subjugated role of homemaker. There was no outcry for women's liberation, or at least not a loud-enough one to attract much attention. There was merely a stubborn refusal on the part of a large number of women to retreat the way they had come.

For one thing there was not as much incentive to run back home to resume housewife and mother roles as there might have been even a few years earlier. Labor-saving devices, such as automatic washers and dryers, vacuum cleaners with attachments that cleaned furniture and walls as well as floors, and a host of other automatic appliances had lessened the drudgery of housework so that women now had the time to hold outside jobs. In addition, in a world rapidly becoming frightened by the population explosion (world population passed 4 billion in April 1976), women who produced more than two children were beginning to be frowned upon instead of being applauded, making the sanctity of motherhood less and less appealing to young women.

Women's growing insistence during the postwar period on being allowed room in the marketplace for jobs was the real beginning of today's movement for women's liberation. But in the beginning it went largely unrecognized, even by the very women making the most stir, as a movement of any sort, let alone as a movement for women's rights. Women merely wanted jobs, and men merely became belligerently aware that women were "trying to take the bread from their mouths." Male resistance was tremendous. Trade unions refused membership to women. Industry, which during the war had proudly publicized that its new force of women workers had lower accident rates than men, now began to bar them from shops on the grounds that the work was too dangerous.

Resistance to change tends to be stereotyped. Just as the rednecks during the civil-rights movement railed against "uppity niggers" who refused to keep their places, male chauvinists complained of pushy women who refused to keep their places, their places being in the home doing the laundry, cooking meals, and raising children.

But in large numbers women continued to refuse to go home, eventually most of the male protest died down, and the economy managed to absorb most of the women who wanted to work without putting hordes of men on the unemployment insurance rolls. A large step toward women's liberation had been taken, though most of the country, including women, was not aware that the change had anything to do with women's rights.

In the years immediately prior to World War II the percentage of women in the civilian labor force had hovered around 23 percent. In 1940 there were 13,783,000 women working. By 1947, when the economy had readjusted from the war years, and most working women who had intended to drop out of the working force after the emergency was over had done so, 16,664,000 were employed. During the next twenty years the number of working women increased by 70 percent, to 28,300,000, while the male working force rose by only 15 percent (from 42,700,000 to 48,987,000). Women still comprised only 37 percent of the labor force (excluding the armed forces and persons confined to institutions but also employed for pay, either within them or on work-release programs), but by 1974 that had risen to 39 percent, with 35,825,000 women working.

As more women entered the labor market, the profile of the typical woman worker changed. According to Department of Labor statistics, in 1900 she was 26 years old and unmarried, in 1940 32 years old and more likely to be unmarried than married, today she is 41 and usually married.

The changing attitude of society toward the working

woman is largely responsible for her changed profile. Prior to World War II tradition discouraged married women from seeking jobs (except for trained professionals, such as teachers, nurses, and social workers), unless economic necessity required them to support their families. A working wife was regarded by the average blue-collar worker as an affront to his masculinity, an advertisement that he was incapable of supporting his family. Today the nonworking wife without small children is likely to be asked by her friends why she doesn't get a job.

Acceptance in the labor market has not meant automatic equality of treatment, though. In 1952 Simone de Beauvoir published a book titled *The Second Sex*, which documented the discriminations still practiced against women despite the Nineteenth Amendment and their apparent new freedom. Among other discriminations, she pointed out that women were still largely restricted to jobs of low responsibility, routinely saw less qualified and less capable men promoted over them, and usually received lower pay than men for doing the same work. The book created no great stir. The majority of women continued under the misapprehension that they had attained all the freedom they were entitled to.

It was another decade before the current revolution really began, and it didn't attain its full strength until the early 1970's. In a sense it gained impetus by hanging on to the coattails of the civil-rights movement. And that, in turn, was an outgrowth of opposition to the Viet Nam War. Probably the black-liberation movement could not have progressed as rapidly as it did without the angry assistance of the campus youth of the 1960's. Originally consolidated by opposition to the Viet Nam War, college and university students nationwide were already aroused and organized for protest when they found another cause in fighting for racial equality.

That fight can't be separated entirely from women's liberation, because it was while the nation was being jarred into awareness of its heartless discrimination against minority groups that women began to demand reexamination of their status in society. The timing was perfect, because it was the first time in history that the majority was in a mood to listen to their complaints.

Even though it began to listen, the general public remained largely unaware that a social upheaval as great as the civil-rights movement was taking place until it actually had taken place. That's about par for the course. The Roman Empire had been declining for over two hundred years before its imminent collapse was abruptly brought to its citizens' attention in A.D. 410 by the Visigoths' sacking and burning of Rome, sixty-six years before the arbitrary date of 476 usually given for the fall of the Roman Empire. The American public wasn't as slow on the uptake as the Romans, but it did take about a decade for the fact to sink in that a quiet revolution had taken place.

It *was* quiet, for the most part, despite the clarion voices of a few leaders. Betty Friedan created considerable stir with her 1963 book *The Feminine Mystique*, which cataloged the ways in which the male numerical minority subtly but systematically suppressed the female majority. Germaine Greer expanded the theme in her 1971 *The Female Eunuch*, and held a much-publicized debate with male chauvinist Norman Mailer, which most observers felt she won. The National Organization for Women was formed and grew to have more than 250 chapters throughout the country. Women's liberation advocates marched and gave speeches denouncing male chauvinism and demanding equal rights. There was a good deal of

publicity about bra burning, but there is only one authen-
ticated record of any such event actually having taken
place.

Most members of the great middle class, both male and
female, simply went about their business while all this
was going on. The men tended to consider the whole
thing a tempest in a teapot that would eventually die out,
like all fads. Many women, possibly the majority, agreed
with their men that the feminists were too shrill, and
decided they wanted no part of the movement. But at the
same time they were reading Friedan and Greer and were
recognizing that they *were* being exploited by a numerical
minority. Most of them attended no women's liberation
rallies, or even spoke out about their discovery, except in
casual conversations with friends. But all of a sudden
millions of them began taking quiet action to express a
newfound sense of personal worth. Housewives began
going back to school. They began studying issues and
examining candidates' qualifications before voting, instead of merely asking their husbands whom to vote for.
Women began to apply for traditional male jobs, and to
charge sex discrimination if they were not given consideration. They began demanding, and sometimes suing for,
equal pay in jobs where they did the same work as men.
They began running for public office and getting elected.

The social revolution was essentially as quiet as the
economic revolution. The majority of women rejected the
radical view of the more vocal feminists that chivalry was
nothing but another device to keep women in subservient
positions, and that the traditional male courtesies, such as
opening doors and giving up seats on buses, should be
discontinued. Most women liked these courtesies, but
they were no longer willing to give up basic rights in
return for them. Quite suddenly large numbers of women

began balking at the double standard that decreed women could not smoke on the street, must wait for men to phone instead of phoning them for dates, must accept male infidelity but remain faithful themselves, and must conform to a host of other discriminatory social rules. Without making a great deal of noise about it, they began breaking many of the male-set taboos and, in effect, calmly letting men know that if they had any objections, they could stop opening doors.

By the time the male population—or even the female population, for that matter—began to realize what an enormous social change was occurring, it had occurred. Feminists say the revolution is by no means over, any more than the fight for racial equality is fully won, but both have made such tremendous advances that at least there is light at the ends of both tunnels. There is still a good deal of male chauvinism, just as there still exists a subtle type of racism that continues to keep most blacks out of white residential neighborhoods. For example, in mid-April 1976 TV newsmen Chuck Ashman and Charles Rowe devoted portions of their nightly Metro News broadcasts out of Los Angeles on two separate evenings to an exposé of how stores and credit agencies still deliberately discriminate against women in granting credit.

But there are also signs that more and more men not only sympathize with the women's liberation movement, but actively approve of it. Around the same time as the Ashman-Rowe broadcasts, Unitarian Minister Lex Crane of Santa Barbara, California, told the congregation a good time to meditate was while performing menial tasks requiring little concentration. When, to give an example, he said, "A housewife could do this while doing the dishes, or a husband while mowing the lawn," there was a murmur of objection from the whole congregation, both male and female, at this stereotype designation of sex roles. Pausing and smiling, the minister acknowledged his gaffe by adding, "Or vice versa."

What will be the future of the women's liberation movement? With the progress already made, it seems likely American women will eventually attain an equality of status similar to that already enjoyed by women in Communist countries. In Russia women are accepted into any profession or trade on an equal basis with men. There are as many female plant managers as male ones, and more female physicians. But—and this is a large "but"— there are fewer women in positions of political power than in the United States. They are equally scarce in other Communist countries, including the People's Republic of China. For all their propaganda about the equality of the sexes, the Communist rulers, all male, show no intention of turning over to women any real power.

There is probably a limit at which American men will also balk. Historical evidence seems to indicate that men are so constituted that they will fight to maintain at least a slight edge of superiority, even if intellectually in agreement with the principle of sexual equality. In the 1930's anthropologist Margaret Mead made a study of three different primitive tribes in New Guinea. Among the mountain-dwelling Arapesh, both sexes behaved in the gentle manner in which tradition says women should behave. Among the river-dwelling Mundugumor (a cannibal tribe), both sexes practiced the aggressive kind of behavior which in our culture has generally been approved only for males. Among the lake-dwelling Tchambuli, what we consider customary roles were completely reversed. The men were gossipy, curled their hair, and did the equivalent of shopping together when they traded with other tribes. The women were brisk, managerial, and wore no decorations. In all three tribes the male role was regarded by both sexes as the more important one. Mead's conclusion was that regardless of what accepted male behavior may be, it is considered by society as the higher-status behavior.

Years later, in her book *Male and Female*, published in 1949, Mead said:

> In every known human society, the male's need for achievement can be recognized. Men may cook, or weave, or dress dolls, or hunt humming birds, but if such activities are appropriate occupations of men, then the whole society, men and women alike, votes them as important. When the same occupations are performed by women, they are regarded as less important.

Whether American women can eventually overcome this apparently inherent need for recognition by men, and the apparently equally inherent willingness of women to give it to them, remains to be seen. They have one advantage over women in Communist countries in that they can reach any political office if they can talk enough people into voting for them. With their numerical majority they could sweep all public offices if they ever organized as a solid bloc.

It is interesting to conjecture what would happen in that unlikely event. What probably wouldn't happen is any great improvement over the way things are now run by men. That wars would end if women ruled the world is a pleasant fantasy hardly supported by historical record. The English queens have been as ruthless and warmongering as any rulers in history. Catherine the Great of Russia, mother of a dozen children, spent a good part of her reign waging wars of conquest in an insatiable hunger to expand her empire. More recently, Indira Gandhi of India and former Prime Minister Golda Meir of Israel have shown no hesitancy to lead their respective nations into war.

We have already seen in previous chapters that women are as capable of horrendous crimes as are men. Placed in positions of political leadership, there is no reason to believe their behavior would be any less horrendous than that of our past male leaders. It has always been assumed by science-fiction writers that if the world is ever destroyed in a nuclear holocaust, some male ruler will push the button that starts the final war. But if it does ever happen, a woman could be the button-pusher.

Chapter 7

The Delinquent Girl

The famous English jurist Sir William Blackstone (1723–1780) reported in *Commentaries on the Law of England* the conviction of an eight-year-old boy for setting fire to some barns "with malice, revenge and cunning." The child was hanged. In 1828 a thirteen-year-old boy was hanged in New Jersey for a crime committed when he was twelve.

Even in an age when severe punishment of criminals was common, these were uncommon incidents. In both England and America common law held that children under seven could not be guilty of crimes because they were incapable of guilty minds (mens rea). Children between seven and fourteen were likewise considered to be innocent of criminal intent, unless they were intelligent enough to understand the nature of their acts and could distinguish between right and wrong. Thus the eight-year-old and the thirteen-year-old were executed because they were brighter than average.

Aside from the limited protection of these two legal principles, prior to 1899 children received no different treatment than adults before the bar of justice. Though executions of eight-year-olds and thirteen-year-olds were not common, the hanging of teenagers fifteen and up was.

It was not until 1899 that the principle of treating juvenile offenders differently from adult criminals was born, although some scattered efforts in that direction had been made earlier. In 1825 New York State established the House of Refuge, the first reformatory in the United States. Children were still tried, convicted and sentenced before the same tribunals as adults, but now they were incarcerated with other children instead of in penitentiaries with adult criminals. Several other states followed suit, although slowly. By 1847 only New York, Pennsylvania, and Massachusetts had reformatories. In the 1870's Massachusetts provided for the separate trial of children, although they were still tried under the same criminal laws as adults. New York, Rhode Island, and Indiana soon passed similar laws, but in the other states and territories children continued to be tried along with adults and to be sentenced to the same penitentiaries.

The first juvenile court in history was established in Chicago in 1899 by an Illinois law titled "An act to regulate the treatment and control of dependent, neglected and delinquent children." The law propounded the revolutionary principle that juvenile lawbreakers were no longer to be considered criminals, but were merely to be declared wards of the state, subject to the guardianship and control of the juvenile court. They were to be treated essentially the same as dependent and neglected children, who already were regarded as special wards of the state, and over whom the courts had long exercised a sort of parental control.

Within ten years nineteen other states plus the District of Columbia had passed similar laws. By 1920 forty-five states had such laws, and today there are juvenile court systems in all fifty states.

The theory behind the juvenile justice system is

humanitarian. The juvenile court judge, instead of being an ogre to mete out punishment, was to act as a sort of foster father, his primary concern to be the welfare of the child. This is an admirable idea, but like many idealistic concepts, it hasn't worked out as intended. Unfortunately many juvenile court judges not only make poor surrogate fathers, but according to *Christian Science Monitor* reporter Howard James, they don't even make good judges. In his 1970 book, *Children in Trouble: A National Scandal*, he reveals that juvenile court judgeships are widely regarded by those in the legal profession as the least desirable of judicial appointments, with the result that too often they go to the least-competent candidates available for the bench. James expresses the blunt opinion that ". . . very, very few [juvenile] judges are qualified for the job they do." Since, in gathering material for his book, James visited forty-four states, investigating juvenile courts, detention facilities, and reform schools, his opinion has to be given some weight. Though he notes that there are some good juvenile court judges and even a few outstanding ones, he backs up his contention with case history after case history of bad ones, often giving names. He charges that most of these judges act as dictators over the lives of the children who come before them and, far from considering their welfare, use their positions to enforce their own personal ideas of morality on their powerless wards.

In his 1969 book *The Child Savers: The Invention of Delinquency*, University of California Criminologist Anthony M. Platt goes even further. He says that the pretense that the juvenile justice system was established to protect young people from the harsh treatment of adult courts is pure hypocrisy, and that the real purpose of the founders of the system was to ensure the "normal" behavior of youths, to oversee their attitudes to authority, their family relationships, and their morality. The adults who dreamed up the idea, according to Platt, assumed that all children must be dependent, and that parental authority was a divine right. So they created a special court to prevent "premature" independence and to monitor and enforce traditional sex roles.

Whether or not that was the purpose of those who originally thought up the system, there is considerable evidence that this philosophy rules the system today, particularly insofar as girls are concerned. In 1975, 380,067 girls under 18 were arrested. Though 132,016 of these arrests were for serious crimes, the majority were for offenses that would not even be classed as crimes if the girls had been adults.

Vedder and Somerville, authors of *The Delinquent Girl*, sent a questionnaire to the superintendents of all public training schools for juvenile delinquents listed in the *Directory of Public Training Schools,* published by the U.S. Department of Health, Education and Welfare. The questionnaire covered a variety of matters, but one question involved the reasons for which girls had been committed to those schools. Regardless of geographic location, the three most common offenses, in order of importance, were running away, incorrigibility, and sex delinquency, none of which the girls could have been arrested for if they had been adults.

Reckless and Kay, the authors of the section of the 1967 *Report of the President's Commission on Law Enforcement and the Administration of Justice* titled "The Female Offender," wrote: "More than one-half of the girls referred to the juvenile courts in 1965 were referred for conduct that would not be criminal if committed by adults."

Reckless and Kay listed much the same type of noncriminal offenses as Vedder and Somerville, but not in quite the same order. They agreed with Vedder and Somerville that running away and incorrigibility were the two top offenses, but included waywardness and truancy as next important before sexual delinquency, followed by ungovernability and "being in need of supervision."

Only 20 percent of the boys arrested were charged with such noncriminal acts, they noted.

In a study of juvenile offenders in Honolulu, Dr. Meda Chesney-Lind, who teaches sociology at Honolulu Community College, found that 70 percent of all girls in that city referred to court were charged with juvenile offenses, compared to 31 percent of the boys.

This double standard of treatment by the juvenile justice system parallels the attitude of the average parent. American parents have always exercised closer control over the activities of girls than of boys in an effort to protect their daughters' virtue. Chesney-Lind says, "A 'good' girl is never sexual, although she must be sexually appealing, while a healthy boy must prove his masculinity by experimenting sexually. The [juvenile] courts, therefore, often operate under two sets of juvenile-delinquency laws, one for boys and one for girls. They reserve their harshest and most paternalistic treatment for girls."

The juvenile justice system reflects traditional parental philosophy by meting out punishment to girls who defy parental authority or violate society's sexual mores. Parents report errant daughters to the police much more readily than they report sons. They seldom send police looking for sons who stay out all night, but it is common for them to have their daughters arrested for such violations of parent-set curfews.

The concern of the law with runaways is understandable. Many juvenile girls are forced into prostitution in order to survive. Many young people of both sexes are the victims of crimes. In August 1973 the graves of twenty-seven boys murdered by a trio of thrill killers were unearthed in Houston, Texas. Most of the boys were runaways. As a direct result of this incident, Congress passed the Runaway Youth Act, which became law in August 1974. It provided for shelters to be established in key cities, staffed with youth counselors, and for a national toll-free switchboard in Chicago to which runaways may call to get in touch with their parents. It handles about a thousand calls a month.

New York City is so concerned with the noncriminal offense of running away from home that there is a special Police Department Runaway Unit that patrols the streets looking for runaway minors. In New York State a minor is subject to paternal control only until age 16. In other states the age ranges from 16 to 18. An interstate agreement provides for the law of the minor's home state to apply. New York law says a minor must show identification to a police officer on demand, and if a person cannot produce proof of not being a minor, he or she may be held as a John Doe or Jane Doe for investigation. A child may be held for only seventy-two hours without a hearing, but a family court judge may order more or less indefinite detention while the Runaway Unit contacts police departments around the country in an attempt to learn if the child is a runaway.

About 77 percent of the runaways caught by the Runaway Unit are girls, and about 57 percent are from out of state. There is no way to verify the guess, but it is the belief of Sergeant James Greenlay, who heads the unit, that the 77 percent figure is not necessarily because more girls run away, but because fewer runaway boys are reported by their parents. It is also possible, of course, although the sergeant would probably deny it, that the paternalism apparent throughout the juvenile justice system operates here as well. Perhaps members of the unit unconsciously tend to be more on the lookout for runaway girls than for runaway boys.

Greenlay estimates that at any given moment there are as many as twelve thousand runaway children in New York City, but only about 1 percent of this number is ever apprehended by his unit.

Though the concern of society for runaway children is understandable, it seems to result in as much unfair treatment as it does in protection. Large numbers of children are not simply rebelling against parental authority when they run away, but are fleeing miserable or even dangerous family situations. Greenlay reports that it is not unknown for a parent to whom he phones the news that a missing daughter has been found to tell him, "We don't want her back." He cites one case where a fifteen-year-old North Carolina girl left home because her drunken father fired a gun at her. Yet such children often end up in institutions which, regardless of euphemistic titles such as Training School for Girls, are essentially jails, simply because they sought escape from intolerable situations.

Judge J. McNary Spigner of Columbia, South Carolina, is one of the few outstanding juvenile court judges cited by James in his study. Judge Spigner is quite aware of the injustices imposed on many children by the system, and he is equally aware of his powerlessness to correct all of them. In a 1969 case he let some of his frustration show in his commitment order to reform school of a thirteen-year-old girl who left home because of abuse by an alcoholic mother. He decreed:

> This court has no place for this child. It cannot find a foster home that will accept her. It has no home of its own

where this child can stay. So she is committed to the School for Girls, which in this instance is being used as an orphanage. Substantially, the child is being punished for the misdeeds of her mother. The court knows this is wrong, but it has no alternative.

The statutes establishing juvenile court systems in the various states have consistently followed the principle that such courts are not criminal courts, but are places where the problems of young people may be worked out by surrogate fathers (the judges) with sympathy and understanding, and with the welfare of the troubled children always in mind. The usual rules of courtroom procedure and the constitutional rights assured adults charged with crimes were therefore deemed to be unnecessary. The theory was that children were not on trial in these courts, but were merely attending informal hearings before kindly father figures whose sole interest was to help them. So that children would be protected from the stigma of having their misdeeds aired publicly, hearings were held in private.

The glaring fault with this idealistic reasoning is that it took no account of human nature. Perhaps if all juvenile court judges were kindly father figures, the courts would work as designed. But in fact most juvenile court judges run their courts as though they were criminal courts whose purpose is to punish wrongdoers. Too many judges have construed the informal rules as license to convict and sentence children on any evidence they please—or sometimes on no evidence—for a variety of vague offenses that probably would be ruled unconstitutional if they were tested in adult courts.

To illustrate the omnibus nature of some statutes dealing with juvenile delinquency, here is the definition of a delinquent child given in the original 1899 Illinois statute establishing the first juvenile court in history:

... a delinquent child is any male who while under the age of 17 years, or any female while under the age of 18 years, violates any law of this State; or is incorrigible, or knowingly associates with thieves, vicious or immoral persons; or without just cause or without consent of its parents, guardian or custodian absents itself from its home or place of abode, or is growing up in idleness or crime; or knowingly frequents a house of ill repute; or knowingly frequents any policy shop or place where any gambling device is operated; or frequents any saloon or dram shop where intoxicating liquors are sold; or patronizes or visits any public pool room or bucket shop; or wanders about any railroad yards or tracks or jumps or attempts to jump onto any moving train; or habitually wanders about the streets in the nighttime without being on any lawful business or lawful occupation; or enters any car or engine without lawful authority; or uses vile, obscene, vulgar or indecent language in any public place or about any school house; or is guilty of indecent or lascivious conduct.

Obviously under this definition virtually any child could be found delinquent if the court chose to make that finding. Even more modern statutes are full of such vague terms as "willful disobedience," "incorrigibility," "stubbornness," and "associating with vicious persons."

Under such vague laws countless children have been tried, convicted, and sentenced to reform schools in all fifty states, the District of Columbia, and in United States territories, without the right of trial by jury, the right of counsel, the right to confront and cross-examine the persons bringing charges against them, or any of the other constitutional rights guaranteed adults.

In 1964 a juvenile named Gerald Gault was arrested in Arizona on the complaint of a Mrs. Cook that he had made an obscene phone call to her. Gerald's parents, both of whom were at work when the arrest was made, were not informed of the arrest and only learned of it that evening when they began inquiring among Gerald's friends because he had not come home. When they finally tracked him down at the Detention Home, a probation officer told them why he had been arrested and that a hearing would be held the next day.

Mrs. Cook did not attend the hearing. Aside from the judge and Gerald, only Gerald's mother, a brother, and two probation officers were present. (Gerald was already on probation for a previous offense.) No sworn testimony was heard, and no transcript of the trial testimony was made. After informally questioning Gerald about the alleged phone call, the judge remanded him to custody pending his decision. Three days later Gerald was released without explanation, but three days after that another hearing was called. Again Mrs. Cook did not attend. Because at that hearing there was contradictory testimony as to whether Gerald or a friend of his named Ronald had made the phone call, Gerald's mother asked the court to call Mrs. Cook to testify. The judge ruled that this was unnecessary, found that Gerald was a juvenile delinquent, and committed him to the State Industrial School until he reached the age of twenty-one.

Gerald's parents fought the case all the way to the United States Supreme Court, which handed down the landmark Gault decision in 1967. In it the Court gave juveniles charged with offenses the right of receiving notice of the precise charges against them sufficiently in advance of hearings to allow reasonable time to prepare defense, the right to counsel, the right to confront and cross-examine their accusers, and the right to be advised of their privilege against self-incrimination.

In his study, news reporter Howard James found that the decision had little impact on many juvenile courts, which went right on operating in the same old way. He found that an appalling number of juvenile-court judges had not read the decision, a few had never even heard of it, and that many who were aware of its provisions were simply ignoring it. How such judges manage to maintain their self-righteous insistence that children obey the law while they break it themselves is puzzling.

In recent years the American Bar Association and the Institute of Judicial Administration have both become so concerned over the inadequacies of the juvenile justice system that they created a joint commission to study the matter and recommend improvements. The appointed body, which has the rather imposing title of the Joint Commission of the Juvenile Justice Standards Project, took four years to complete the study. The results and recommendations are being released in a series of volumes, ultimately to number more than twenty, which began to be published in 1976.

United States Appellate Judge Irving R. Kaufman, cochairman of the Joint Commission, recently gave a capsule preview of the findings that was highly critical of the present system. He said:

> For too long now, this nation's juvenile justice system has hidden its woefully inadequate performance behind lofty aspirations and wishful dreams . . . the juvenile justice system has failed to protect the juvenile from society or society from the violent child. The recent increase in juvenile crime and the criminalization of the young by so-called "noncriminal" institutions have made the public painfully aware that our juvenile courts have failed to fulfill the purpose of their creation.

The four-year project was staffed by experts in law, psychiatry, psychology, sociology, penology, and a number of other disciplines. According to Judge Kaufman its recommendations will be wide-ranging and will involve comprehensive changes in all the institutions charged with the administration of juvenile justice.

All juveniles who appear in juvenile court are not merely helpless victims of an unfair system, of course. As previously mentioned, in 1975 there were 132,016 girls under 18 arrested for serious crimes compared to 581,904 boys in the same year. And, as with adult criminals, the rate of increase of girls' crimes is far higher than that of boys'. From 1960 to 1975 serious crimes by boys under 18 increased by 117.4 percent, but those committed by girls jumped 425.4 percent. In the single year from 1974 to 1975 the boys' rate went up 2.5 percent, the girls', 3.9 percent. So, despite the fact that boys committed nearly four and a half times as many serious crimes as girls that year, the gap is steadily closing. In 1960 boys were committing nearly ten times as many Part I crimes as girls.

Youthful crime has even moved in off the street right into the classroom. In December 1975 New York City School Chancellor Irving Anker released a report showing a 55 percent increase in crime within the public schools over the previous year. During the first three months of the academic year, there were 289 assaults on teachers and 173 robberies of teachers, students, and others on school grounds. The same day that report was released, three hundred teachers and educational researchers from all over the country were meeting in Washington, D.C., to explore the causes and possible solutions to crime in the schools, the national cost of which they estimated to be $600 million a year. It sounded more like a convention of prison wardens than a conference of educators, with the discussion covering such matters as security guards, weapons, motion-monitoring systems, and other devices designed to reduce crimes by schoolchildren within the schools.

In New York City the police know of 278 male youth gangs, 23 of which have female auxiliaries. In addition there are 13 known all-female gangs, which engage in essentially the same types of activity as boys' gangs. They congregate at night on street corners, flaunt drinking in public, deliberately shock passersby with profanity, steal, vandalize, and have fights with members of rival all-girl gangs.

These gang girls are in no sense "liberated" however. They accept subservience to boys as the natural order of things. The members of the girls' auxiliary of one New York gang proudly wear lettered on their jackets: "Property of the Savage Nomads." Walter B. Miller says of the Molls, the all-girl gang described in Chapter 5:

> The evidence is clear that the Molls and other young women like them not only did not resent the fact that their status was directly dependent on that of the boys, but actively sought this condition and gloried in it. The Molls accepted without question a declaration by one of the Hoods that "they ain't nuthin' without us, and they know it."

Nevertheless these female children can be dangerous, and often they are vicious. Prior to her research for *Sisters in Crime*, Dr. Freda Adler was research coordinator for the Addiction Science Center affiliated with Temple University, and she spent some time studying female gangs in the ghetto sections of several Pennsylvania cities. She says:

> The girls are as young as 13 and range to 18. They meet in cellar clubs, homes, empty lots, anywhere. And they are violent. They steal from stores, snatch purses and, when the mood or need arises, go on the attack against vulnerable passersby, mostly elderly persons who cannot resist.

In 1975 there were 7,774 girls under 18 arrested for the violent crimes of murder, robbery, and aggravated assault, an increase of 74.2 percent over the five-year period since 1970. The increase over 1960 was 503.5 percent. Girls committed more than four times as many murders and nonnegligent manslaughters in 1975 as in 1960. (Manslaughter by negligence involves no intent to kill, but merely criminal carelessness, such as running down a pedestrian while driving drunk. Nonnegligent manslaughter may or may not involve intent to kill, but involves at least intent to harm.)

As alarming as these statistics are, it would be false to assume that the country is overrun by killer young girls. Actual arrests in recent years of girls under 18 for murder and nonnegligent homicide average only between 100 and 150 a year, whereas between 1,000 and 1,500 boys are arrested for such crimes during the same time span. Despite a general year-to-year increase of violent crimes by juvenile girls, this particular crime has been staying fairly stable, with minor fluctuations. In 1975 131 juvenile girls were arrested for murder and nonnegligent manslaughter. The previous year, although violent crimes in general jumped by 16 percent from 1973 to 1974 for juvenile girls, murder and nonnegligent homicide dropped by 7.1 percent. The increase from 1972 to 1973 had been 8.6 percent, however.

The low numerical number of such crimes is hardly reassuring, though. Even 100 female children committing murder each year is an alarming thought.

Chapter 8

The Black Female Criminal

The pattern of criminality among black women has been consistently different from that among white women, although the two now are beginning to converge toward the same point. For that matter, the pattern of criminality among black men has also differed from that of white men.

Unfortunately the statistical data for both are mixed together. Although FBI statistics break down arrests by race as well as by sex, they do not break down each sex by race, or vice versa. There is therefore no way to tell from the charts how many of the women arrested are black, or how many of the blacks arrested are women. However, it is apparent that blacks, women and men together, commit a disproportionate number of serious crimes, and actually surpassed whites in violent crimes. In 1975 blacks, who comprise only 11 percent of the population, committed 32.8 percent of the serious crimes and nearly 50 percent of the violent crimes. They committed 1,676 more murders than whites did, and 21,269 more robberies. But there were 33,866 fewer aggravated assaults, and 1,364 fewer forcible rapes.

Though FBI figures do not make a race-sex breakdown,

there have been some other studies which indicate that more black women than white ones are arrested. One national survey, for instance, showed that 53 percent of the women arrested for prostitution were black. There has never been a national survey to determine the proportion of black women arrested for serious crimes, but a number of regional studies indicate the majority of women committing these are also black. If prison population is any indication, black women surpass white women in criminality, because more than half the inmates are black.

There are probably several reasons for the higher rate of criminality among both black men and women. Blacks in general live on a lower economic level than whites, most of them are still crowded together in urban ghettos despite fair-housing laws, and in many cases they have a different family structure than whites. Some black leaders charge that a large factor is simply that police more readily arrest blacks and that the white-dominated judicial system consistently treats them more harshly.

There is some evidence to support the charge. When the United States Supreme Court ruled on July 2, 1976 that the death penalty was again constitutional under certain conditions (overturning its own 1972 ruling banning it as "cruel and unusual punishment") there were 610 persons on Death Rows across the country; 310 were black.

The ruling was on test cases from five different states. It upheld the death laws in Florida, Georgia and Texas, and struck down those in Louisiana and North Carolina. In the 14 states with death laws similar to those approved by the Supreme Court, presumably the way is now clear to execute the 310 persons on Death Rows there, although there will almost certainly be further appeals. In the 20 states with death laws similar to those of Louisiana and North Carolina, the laws are apparently void.

At the time of the Supreme Court decision, North Carolina alone had nearly one fifth of all those awaiting execution in the country (122), including two of the ten women under death sentence. One of those was black, the other American Indian. North Carolina also has the distinction of having legally executed more blacks than any other state in the union. In the past the state has executed 282 blacks, compared to 73 whites. The only two women ever executed in North Carolina were black.

Taking the other factors one at a time, in July 1975 the United States Census Bureau published the results of a *Study of the Social and Economic Status of the Black Population*, which showed that black families' median income for 1974 was only 58.5 percent that of whites'. It also showed a 9.9 percent unemployment rate among blacks, as compared to 5 percent among whites.

Since the Ford administration had admitted a 9 percent overall unemployment figure, the Census Bureau figure has to be suspect. The Urban League, which may tend to exaggerate in the other direction, puts the black unemployment figure for 1975 at 26 percent, and the rate among black male youths at 43 percent. The League also estimates that over 680,000 unemployed blacks are ineligible for unemployment insurance. With that many frustrated young black people, perhaps we should wonder why there aren't even more crimes committed by them.

The effect on the crime rate of people being jammed together in ghettos is obvious. Wherever there is a combination of poverty, crowded living conditions, and few recreational outlets, a high crime rate can be expected. One of the reasons the majority of black criminals' victims are also black is that the majority of black crime takes place in the urban ghettos. It is not a matter of selectivity on the part of the criminals, but merely that in their environment they come into contact with far more blacks than whites.

The differing structure between black and white families is not credited by sociologists as a cause of the higher crime rate among blacks in general, but only as one explanation of the higher rate among black women. The theory is that the socioeconomic roles of black males and females are much closer than between white males and females, and that consequently there is less difference in their criminal behavior. A staff report submitted to the National Commission on the Causes and Prevention of Violence in December 1969 by Donald J. Mulvihill, Melvin M. Tumin, and Lynn A. Curtis reads in part:

> It can be shown . . . that where the cultural roles of women and men come to resemble each other, their criminal rates also come closer together. Numerous observers have commented on the great similarity in the roles of lower class Negro males and females as compared with their peers in the white group. Data show that the rates of deviant behavior of Negro lower class males and females are closer than are those of comparable groups in the white population.

The "numerous observers" cited above may have included Edwin H. Sutherland and Donald R. Cressey, who in their 1966 *Principles of Criminology* wrote: "In the United States the sex ratio is less extreme among Negroes than it is among whites, and it is probable that Negro males and females more closely resemble each other in social standing than do white males and females."

Daniel P. Moynihan once characterized black families as matriarchal, deviant, and unstable, which managed to rouse the ire of a number of black leaders. There is some evidence that at least the first charge is true, however, although even that is contested by many black sociologists and even by some white ones. Frances Lucas, a black woman who is a program supervisor for the New York City Bureau of Child Guidance, wrote in the 1975 Spring issue of *Mental Hygiene:*

> Black women have never been sheltered or overprotected by their men. Indeed, their men were robbed of this right by society. From the beginning of the duality of races in America, black men could not protect themselves nor their family. Black male aggression was associated with oversexuality and uncurbed physical strength—both of which were intolerable. White society thought that emasculation was necessary for control, and it did a good job of that. Therefore, it was often a choice of accepting an emasculated timid role or death. Often, the woman protected her husband and her children, and—despite the concerted effort of some parts of white America to destroy black family life—held the family together. This is the image of misunderstood strong matriarchy. The black woman never developed this pattern in relation to the black man, but it was in relation to society. The typical intact black family is not matriarchal.

Lucas' argument seems to split hairs, in that it commends the strength of the black woman in virtually single-handedly holding her family together while at the same time denying that she heads it. Regardless of whether you call her a matriarch or merely a courageous woman, the fact remains that the black woman far more frequently heads her family than her white sister. The previously mentioned Census Bureau report shows that in 1975 there were 35.3 percent of all black families headed by women, compared to only 10.5 percent among whites. During the depression years there were estimates, largely based on welfare statistics, that in the major northern cities as many as 60 percent of Negro households were headed by women.

Lucas describes rather vividly what brought this about, but her description can stand the embellishment of some examples. I'll cite three from my own personal experience.

Like most middle-class whites who have felt guilt over white America's treatment of blacks, over the years I have observed countless wrongs done to blacks for no reason other than their skin color. But these three stand out, all occurring at about two-year intervals during the 1930's.

The first occurred when, as a teenager growing up in St. Louis, I once had to appear in City Court on a traffic charge. One of the cases ahead of mine was a white man who had been charged with forcible rape of a black woman. Ordinarily this would have been a matter for the Circuit Court for Criminal Causes, but the assistant circuit attorney in charge of the case explained to the court that the charge had been reduced to common assault, to which the accused wanted to plead guilty. (Obviously there had been a plea bargain, I realized many years later when I came to know more about court procedure, in which the accused had been offered the reduced charge in return for a guilty plea, but this wasn't mentioned.) The man was sentenced to six months in the City Workhouse.

Coincidentally there happened to be a black man in Death Row at the penitentiary at Jefferson City at that time, awaiting the gas chamber for the forced rape of a white woman.

The second incident occurred when I was a freshman at Central College at Fayette, Missouri, a quiet town of 2,600, more than half black. The whites lived in the center of town, the blacks ringed the white section in run-down houses and shacks. Most of the blacks had the surname of Howard, because they were descendants of the slaves of the largest plantation owner who had lived in that area, whose last name had been Howard. Possibly because it was a remote, off-the-highway community where little change ever took place, the treatment of blacks in Fayette was even more restrictive than in other places in Missouri. Segregation was complete, even to separate drinking fountains at the county courthouse labeled "White" and "Colored."

I had been in school only a short time when the town tough shot and killed a black man on the street, reportedly for not having moved out of his way fast enough. The sheriff arrested the killer for drunk-and-disorderly conduct, and he drew ten days in the county jail. No charge was ever presented to the grand jury, and the incident was never mentioned in the local paper.

Today student activists no doubt would have raised such protest that the grand jury not only would have been forced to indict the killer, but probably would have indicted the sheriff as well. But in the 1930's student passivism was the rule. Although the story circulated through the five hundred students on campus, I don't recall that there was a great deal of discussion about it, or even any particular feeling of injustice. Most of the students were from other localities, and the general attitude seemed to be that local mores were none of their business.

Incidents such as this, as blatantly unjust as they were, probably had less effect on black attitudes toward themselves than a more benign and subtle formative process employed in the Deep South. Such injustices tended more to induce inner rage than submissiveness among blacks, and rage at injustice is more likely to build self-esteem than to destroy it. James Baldwin, in The Fire Next Time, wrote: " . . . rage, hatred and murder, hatred for white men so deep that it often turned against him and his own, and made all love, all trust, all joy, impossible."

The third incident I recall so vividly was of that more benign and subtle type of injustice. A few years after the

Fayette murder I spent part of a summer vacation on a cotton-and-tobacco plantation near Durant, Mississippi, owned by a classmate's father. The Negro workers lived in eight tenant shacks on the place. About sixty people occupied the shacks, two thirds of them workers, the rest either too young or too old to work. In return for free rent, a plot of ground behind each shack for a vegetable garden, a weekly slab of salt pork and $8 a month per family, my classmate's father got his fields tilled, his house kept clean, and his cooking done. (He was a widower.) Apparently he took excellent care of his serfs. He told me that in years when the gardens failed to produce enough, he supplemented their diets with store-bought vegetables. Bolts of cotton for dresses and shirts and bolts of denim for trousers were standard Christmas and birthday presents for the workers. He also assured me that he called the vet for an ailing black as quickly as he called him for a sick horse.

He went to some pains to convince me, as a visitor from the North (Missourians, while not quite Yankees, were definitely northerners to Mississippians) that his relationship with his blacks was more or less standard in the South. The point he obviously meant to make was that blacks in the Deep South not only were not mistreated, but were well cared for. He explained rather proudly, for instance, that the elderly, when they were no longer able to work, were never cast out, but lived out their days under the same protective patronage as the productive workers. At one point he said something that still vividly sticks in my mind: "Any man who'd beat a nigger would be looked down on as bad as though he'd kicked a dog."

This modern feudal system, which in effect simply recreated the slave economy under slightly different rules, extended throughout the Deep South clear up until World

War II, and was accepted as a fact of life by both whites
and blacks. It had a more crushing effect on the black man
than on the black woman, though, because it placed him
in an even more subservient position than it did her. Black
women worked in the fields alongside the men, but at
least some of them were also brought into their masters'
and mistresses' homes to clean and cook, and even to take
care of the children. Whites often felt genuine affection for
their female servants, probably reciprocated in at least
some cases, and with at least pretended reciprocation in
all cases. Black men, being outside workers except in
families rich enough to afford butlers, tended to be held at
a greater distance.

Thus black women had more status in the paternalistic
white society than black men. And because whites set the
rules, they also tended to have more status even in their
own black society. The stereotype black woman was brisk,
efficient, reliable, and a tireless worker. The stereotype
black man was so lazy and unreliable that he constantly
had to be prodded to get any work out of him. On planta-
tions such as that of my classmate's father, these
stereotypes were at least approximately accurate, since
there was little incentive for black field workers to do any
more work then they had to. Confronted with the same
futureless prospect, I doubt that my friend's father would
have shown any more ambition.

Black women found their subservience to whites a degree less humiliating than black men did, because *all*
women, even white ones, had been conditioned throughout history to accept inferiority. But to black men the
situation was just as emasculating as Lucas indicated.
Even in the eyes of their own women they were at the
bottom of the social hierarchy.

Attitudes in the enlightened North differed somewhat,

but were just as devastating to the male black ego. Though by legislative act in most northern states blacks had legal and social equality with whites, in practice there was nothing approaching equal treatment. New York State, for example, for years had a Fair Employment Practices Act on its books, forbidding employers to discriminate in hiring because of race, nationality, or religion. Yet prior to the civil-rights movement, hundreds of plants in industrial communities had never employed a Negro. As a random example, the two largest plants in the industrial city of Dunkirk, New York, Alco Products and the Allegheny Ludlum Steel Corporation, maintained the spotless record of never having a black employee clear up until 1960, despite Dunkirk's having a large black population.

Economic discrimination against black men in the North forced them into the same lower-status role to their wives that they had had in the South. It was much more difficult for them to find even menial jobs than it was for black women, who found wide acceptance as charwomen, hotel maids, and even as factory workers in certain industries, such as canning and clothes making. The ignominy of having to depend on a wife for support, and economic despair in general, drove many a black man to desert his family, forcing black women into the position of heads of households whether they liked it or not.

This is one of the reasons middle-class and lower-class black women find it difficult to become very fired up about women's liberation. They were liberated more than they cared to be years ago. It is hard for them to empathize with the middle-class white woman who wants to throw off the shackles of homemaking and find self-fulfillment in a career outside the home. When the career is scrubbing floors, or endlessly pasting labels on cans of fruit as they move along an assembly line, most black women would gladly trade it for the opportunity of becoming homemakers.

There has been no great flocking to the cause by educated black women either. At the moment they are more concerned with the liberation of their race than with the liberation of women, which to them seems to be primarily a fight to free white women. Thus the current president of the board of the National Association for the Advancement of Colored People is a prominent St. Louis attorney named Margaret Bush-Wilson, but few prominent black women are visible in the women's liberation movement.

Black men seem to have ambivalent feelings about the movement. They tend to sympathize with the goals because they are similar to the goals of the civil-rights movement, and the leaders appeal to them as allies because for the most part they are liberal women who have fought just as valiantly for racial equality as for their own cause. But black men at the same time feel that though black women have been denied equality by white society, they haven't been denied it by *them*, and in fact in the past black women have generally been in a superior position to black men. Cornish Rogers, associate editor of the *Christian Century*, said in an article in the February 13, 1974, issue of that magazine:

Morever, black men find themselves unable to understand or to sympathize with the complaints of bored middle-class housewives who express bitterness over the fact that while the husband goes off each day to his interesting job or profession, the wife is left at home to do menial, unfulfilling household chores. . . . It is safe to say that the majority of employed black married women today would probably prefer to be housewives if their husbands could earn a decent wage. Being "just a housewife" is a devoutly wished-for dream of many black women who by necessity have had to

seek employment outside the home—often to do the housework of bored white women.

There seems to be little doubt that the greater degree of
equality between black males and females is the main
reason for the lesser degree of difference in their crime
rates than among whites. That this lesser gap in criminal
behavior is no recent phenomenon, but has existed for
decades, seems to be the opinion of most sociologists who
have addressed the subject. Since the percentage increase
of crimes committed by blacks (including both sexes) has
approximated the increase by males of all races, it seems
reasonable to assume that the percentage rise of female
criminality among blacks has probably paralleled that of
black males. In short, the black female rate has not risen as
rapidly as the white female rate, simply because the black
female rate was already up there alongside that of men.
Despite the lack of confirming statistics on a national
level, it therefore also seems reasonable to assume that
most of the percentage increase of female criminality in
recent years has been in the white sector.

The relationship between black men and women seems
to be undergoing a subtle but important change as a direct
result of the civil-rights movement, which in turn may
affect the crime rate of black women. Though none of the
three incidents of black suppression I described would be
possible today, the civil-rights war is far from won. Some
of the battles have been won, though, and one of them is
the battle for self-respect. The black man no longer ac-
cepts the inferior role thrust upon him by white society.
The symptoms of his rejection of inferior status have been
visible for more than a decade in such things as the "Black
is beautiful" slogan, Afro hairdos, student demands for
black-studies courses in the colleges and universities,

and in black pressure to revise standard history textbooks to include the roles played by black persons. Such belligerent assertions of self-worth symbolize the changed attitude the black man has of himself. The days when he felt obliged to step off the sidewalk to let whites pass are gone forever. Today, while he still may have trouble getting the job he wants, or moving into the neighborhood he wants, he has no trouble at all looking the white man straight in the eye and proclaiming himself every bit as good a man. That changed image of himself has inevitably changed his image in the eyes of black women as well. And since male chauvinism is not a monopoly of the white race, the black male has become more aggressive in his relationship with women at the same time that he has become more aggressive in his relationship with white society.

Thus at a time when white women are gradually moving toward equality with men, black women are tending to move the other way. Perhaps this is what Frances Lucas was talking about when she said, "The typical intact black family is not matriarchal." It is not likely that black women will recede as far as the inferior position white women found themselves in prior to the women's liberation movement, but then it is not likely either that white women will proceed as far as the black woman did when white society was emasculating her husband. It is probable that both will stop at some equal point short of full equality with men, black women because they refuse to retreat any further, white women because men will refuse to let them advance any further.

Since that opinion is bound to rub the fur of feminists, let me make clear that it is a forecast, not a statement of philosophy. So far as I am concerned, women can take over the running of the world, if they want it. But I doubt very much that men will permit it. Always they will insist on at least a slight edge of superiority. That is quite apparent in the Communist nations, where presumably all sex discrimination has been scrapped. Men there have managed to retain the sizable edge of complete political control. There is no reason to believe that American men will be any more generous in sharing power.

In any event, when black women and white women eventually attain a comparable status in their relationship to men, it is likely that the crime rate for both will balance also.

Chapter 9

The Female Terrorists

The bomb-planting political terrorists of recent years, who nurture the naïve notion that blowing up branch offices of the Bank of America is somehow going to bring about social change, have had no effect whatever on FBI crime statistics. The FBI estimates that there are no more than five hundred hard-core revolutionists throughout the nation in the so-called underground, and only a few of those have ever been arrested. Out of the 9,273,600 criminal arrests in 1975 reported to the FBI by over 13,000 police agencies, these few arrests could not possibly have changed any of the statistical figures by even a minute fraction of 1 percent.

They deserve attention on three counts, though.

First, the FBI statistics show arrests only, not crimes committed, and the terrorists have committed more than their share of violent crimes. During the first five months of 1976 there were 549 bombings in the United States, all but a few believed by the FBI to have been set by terrorist groups. Twenty-three persons were killed, 108 were injured, and property damage was estimated at $6 million. During the most violent period of political terrorist

activity—from roughly January 1969 to the end of 1970—
there were more than 40,000 bombings, attempted bombings, and bomb threats across the nation. Most of these
were by cranks and psychopaths, but it is estimated that at
least 8,000 were meant as political statements by radical
groups. And though most of them were merely threats or
unsuccessful attempts to bomb, there were enough actual
bombings to shake the nation. During one five-day period
in October 1970 explosions blasted the statue of a policeman in Chicago's Haymarket Square, a courtroom in San
Rafael, California, an ROTC building at the University of
Washington in Seattle, an armory in Santa Barbara,
California, and a courthouse in New York City. The underground organization which at that time called itself the
Weatherman took credit for all five bombings. (The name
is thought to have derived from a popular song in the late
1960's titled *Subterranean Homesick Blues*, in which one
line went, "You don't need a weatherman to know which
way the wind blows.")

Second, most of the underground revolutionaries are
female.

Third, insofar as female criminality is concerned, terrorists' activities have monopolized the headlines since
the late 1960's.

For the purposes of this discussion it is necessary to
draw a clear distinction between the underground political revolutionists and the aboveground political activists.
Enough of the aboveground activists have been arrested
on various charges, mainly stemming from marches and
protest demonstrations, to affect FBI statistics. In 1969
there were 4,000 arrests as the result of such protests, in
1970 there were 7,200. But these were for such offenses as
refusal to disperse, shouting obscenities, and, at worst,
throwing rocks at policemen. Such trivial offenses hardly

compare with the bombing in the summer of 1970 that destroyed a mathematics building at the University of Wisconsin, killing an instructor and injuring four other persons.

Today confrontation as a political device has practically disappeared, and the campuses are quiet. What aboveground political activism there is takes the form of circulating petitions, holding public forums, and backing radical candidates for public office. Onetime radicals who believed in confrontation now have modified their stance to preach the doctrine of forcing change by working within the system. Thus we have the spectacle of Tom Hayden, former activist member of the famous Chicago Seven, running for the United States Senate. But underground activity goes on unabated. The bombings continue.

The typical political terrorist in the United States is young, white, well educated, from an upper-middle-class or wealthy family, and female. There are, of course, male members of the various organizations, but women are in the majority. A small percentage of the men are black, but none of the women are except in the Black Liberation Army, which is not really an underground organization, although a number of its members have gone underground because they are wanted for such crimes as bank robbery and murder. Its best-known member, Joanne Chesimard, 27, has been almost constantly either on trial or awaiting trial in recent years for various alleged bank robberies and the alleged murder of a policeman.

Virtually without exception the blacks involved in the predominantly white terrorist groups are from a lower socioeconomic level, have criminal backgrounds, and have been drawn into the groups because white radicals regard them as symbols of the oppression they are fighting against. It has to be suspected that the motivation of these ex-cons is not entirely political. It must be a pleasant surprise for a man who has spent a considerable part of his life in prisons for such crimes as sticking up liquor stores to learn he is not a criminal after all, that, on the contrary, the crime has been on the part of society *against him*. Probably in many cases, or even in most cases, society *has* sinned against him by offering little opportunity to make anything of his life in legal ways, but that doesn't make his metamorphosis from hardened criminal to idealistic revolutionary any more convincing.

The average American is bewildered at what could cause a well-brought-up young lady who has been given every advantage, including an expensive education, to become a bomb-throwing terrorist. Thomas Powers and Lucinda Franks, reporters for United Press International, won a Pulitzer prize in 1971 for answering that question. Their answer was in the form of a series of articles about Diana Oughton, a young member of the Weatherman who accidentally blew up herself and two fellow members while manufacturing a bomb.

Diana grew up in the small town of Dwight, Illinois, the eldest of four daughters of parents as wealthy as those of Patricia Hearst. As a senior at exclusive Bryn Mawr College she saw poverty for the first time when she joined a project in Philadelphia to tutor black ghetto children. Later she went to Guatemala to teach in the small village of Chichicastenango under the auspices of VISA (the Quaker-run Volunteer International Service Assignments). There she saw even worse proverty than in the Philadelphia ghetto, and began to question the values of the upper class in which she had grown up. She watched with resentment as American tourists visiting Chichicastenango squandered enough money in a week to feed a dozen Indian children for a whole year. She met a young Fulbright scholar, in Guatemala to make an economic study, who told her that American economic aid was simply maintaining the wealthy ruling class of that country in power, with none of it trickling down to the poor. (This shouldn't have surprised her, since it has been a common criticism of American foreign aid going clear back to our attempted bolstering of the Chiang Kai-shek regime. During the 1976 presidential campaign Jimmy Carter quoted an adviser as saying, "We should no longer tax the poor people of a rich country to give aid to the rich people in the poor countries.")

When Diana returned to the United States in 1965, she was feeling guilt and unease at her family's wealth while other people were starving. In 1966 she began work on her master's degree in teaching at the University of Michigan at Ann Arbor. She lived on little money and refused help from her father. There she met William Ayres, the son of the president of Commonwealth Edison Company of Chicago, and a budding radical. In the summer of 1968 she accompanied him to Chicago to work at the national headquarters of the Students for a Democratic Society, an organization of student activists with chapters on campuses all over the country, including Ann Arbor. She was there during the national convention of the Democratic Party in August, when police quelled the rioting of youthful demonstrators protesting the Viet Nam War. The unjustified violence of the police enraged her, and she thereafter always referred to the incident as the "police riot."

In the fall Diana and Ayres returned to Ann Arbor, where both began to become progressively more radicalized. When, in June 1969, the SDS split into two opposing factions in an argument over policy, both chose to go with the Weatherman, a small group of extremists who believed the time had come to move into the streets with a "Red Army." Diana had become a committed revolutionist.

She was active in the October 1969 "Days of Rage" in Chicago, a deliberately planned confrontation with police by the Weatherman. The affair was a disappointment to the organization and a relief to the police. Widely publicized in advance, the Weatherman expected up to 10,000 dissident youth to descend on Chicago from all over the nation. About 300 gathered. They went ahead anyway. Clad in helmets and denim jackets, carrying poles with Vietcong flags on them, they charged through the Loop and the Gold Coast area, smashing windows and windshields and storming into classrooms to write revolutionary slogans and obscenities on blackboards. Diana was one of the approximately 200 arrested.

In December 1969 a "Weatherman War Council" was held at Flint, Michigan. This was a four-day open meeting, even more widely publicized in advance than the Days of Rage, to which the Weatherman leaders hoped to draw large numbers of activists from all over the country to join their Red Army. The council was a total failure. Only 400 showed up, and the violent views of the Weatherman not only failed to recruit any new soldiers, but actively turned off most of the visitors. Even those who classed themselves as revolutionaries could not see how random violence and destruction would accomplish the social goals they believed in.

It was so apparent to all concerned that the council was a failure that even as it was still going on, the leaders of the Weatherman met secretly and independently decided that the only course open to them in fighting American imperialism and racism was violence. They voted to make a complete break with society and go underground, from where they would institute a reign of terror.

It was while helping to prepare for that reign of terror that a bomb she was building accidentally exploded in Diana's hands in March 1970. The accident took place in the basement of the $250,000, four-story town house of businessman James Wilkerson in Greenwich Village. Wilkerson's daughter Cathlyn, 25, a member of the Weatherman, and four other members were living there. The explosion killed Diana, 28 at the time, Terry Robbins, and Theodore Gold, and it destroyed the house. Cathlyn Wilkerson, 25, and Kathy Boudin, 26, were also in the house, but miraculously emerged from the rubble unharmed except for torn and blackened clothing. They showered at a neighbor's, borrowed clean clothing from her, and disappeared before the police arrived. In the ruins police found 60 sticks of dynamite, 30 blasting caps, and 4 homemade bombs.

Three years after sharing a Pulitzer prize Lucinda Franks gave even greater insight into what converts young, affluent, and well-educated girls into revolutionaries by recounting some personal experience in the October 1974 issue of Ms. When she was researching the Diana Oughton story with Tom Powers, she was only 23. At Vassar College she had been involved in the civil-rights movement and had belonged to the SDS. After college she had worked for United Press International (UPI) in London for two years, and was just back in the United States. As part of their research, Franks and Powers visited White Panther headquarters in Ann Arbor. She admits that she was impressed by the revolutionary talk of the White Panthers, and by the feeling that these young people were actually *doing something* about the injustices in America. She wondered if it was just an accident that she had slipped into a career in journalism abroad instead of joining the movement at home.

If a girl intelligent enough to share a Pulitzer prize at the age of 23 can in effect say of Diana Oughton, "There, but for the grace of God, go I," what rich family's daughter is immune? Of course Franks was not necessarily thinking of herself as a terrorist, but only as a potential radical activist, but all terrorists are at first only activists. The difference between the radical and the revolutionist is only one of degree, and most young girls who have crossed the line have also been intelligent and educated.

The undeniable fact is that the social injustices that succeed in radicalizing these young women actually exist. White corporate America *does* oppress the poor by refusing to share any portion of its wealth not forced from it. That any single person is allowed to amass such wealth as the late Howard Hughes, whose estate is estimated at $2.3 billion, while children starve in ghettos, is without question criminally unjust. It is understandable that when the daughters of affluence are confronted by such inequities, at least some of them are overwhelmed by guilt at their families' parts in such oppression. Political activism, protest, and confrontations with authority are the sackcloth and ashes to atone for their guilt. If the guilt is a degree deeper, activism becomes radicalism. An additional degree deeper, and it may become terrorism. The great majority of concerned young women who hope to bring about social reforms work for them by quite legal means within the system, but the potential for any of them to become criminals simply because of their ideology is always there to haunt their parents.

The new political terrorism began in this country with the Weatherman, and that organization is still the largest underground group. However, its name has been changed because "Weatherman" seemed inappropriate for an organization that had become predominantly female. Its members now call themselves the Weather Underground.

A few have surfaced from the underground. In January 1975, four and a half years after pleading guilty to a bombing-conspiracy charge, then jumping bail, Swarthmore graduate Jane Alpert tired of the underground life and turned herself in. Three months later Susan Edith Saxe, 26, who was on the FBI's most-wanted list for a 1970 bank robbery, was arrested in Philadelphia. Other arrests include Cameron Bishop and Patricia Swinton, who were among the original members of the Weatherman group to go underground in 1970.

The Weather Underground is believed to consist of around 200 hard-core members, supported by perhaps 4,000 sympathizers who are willing to help them avoid the police, but take no part in their terrorist activities. Only 22 members in addition to those already captured actually have federal arrest warrants out on them, although there are local warrants on some of the others. These include Mark William Rudd, who as SDS chairman helped organize the first student protests at Columbia University in 1968 and later became the first national secretary of the breakaway Weatherman faction; Bernadine Dohrn, believed to be the current leader of the Weather Underground; William Ayres, previously mentioned as a radicalizing influence on Diana Oughton; Cathlyn Wilkerson, in whose town-house basement Diana blew herself up; and Kathy Boudin, who escaped from that catastrophe with Cathlyn Wilkerson.

No other revolutionary group is believed to approach the size of the Weather Underground, or to have as much support from sympathizers. As a matter of fact, it is the only underground revolutionary group believed to be nationwide, the others mainly being centered in California. A few of the lesser organizations are:

The Black Guerrilla Family. Formed within prisons by members of the Black Liberation Army who are imprisoned, it has several hundred members, all inmates, and all male. Since the Black Liberation Army itself is on the East Coast, members released from California prisons tend to gravitate to other underground radical groups. Most are unable to accept the female leadership, though, and eventually drop out of the radical life. A number of released prisoners are known to have been taken in and helped by Manson Family women. It is believed that Charles Manson issued instructions to help them in return for the Black Guerrilla Family's protecting him against attacks by other inmates.

The Tribal Thumb. Centered in Palo Alto, California, and headed by ex-convict Earl Satcher, the organization is estimated to have about 25 members, mostly male. It distributes revolutionary pamphlets and asks financial help from radicals, but a member arrested in the fall of 1975 told police the revolutionary stance is merely a front to justify crimes for profit.

New World Liberation Front. Believed to have about 25 middle-class white members, both male and female, and a few black ex-convicts, the front claims credit for more than two dozen bombings in the San Francisco Bay area and in Sacramento since September 1974. Buildings bombed include offices of General Motors Company, Pacific Gas and Electric Company, and some subsidiaries of ITT Corporation. The organization is believed to have sheltered William and Emily Harris and Patty Hearst for a time. When Patty Hearst repudiated the Symbionese Liberation Army after her capture, the front issued a statement condemning her for returning to the "ruling class vipers."

The Red Guerrilla Family. Thought to be an offshoot of the New World Liberation Front, its size and composition is unknown. It has claimed credit for a number of bombings, including the Berkeley FBI office.

The Chicano Liberation Front. Centered in Los Angeles, it is thought to have only about 15 hard-core members, all Mexican-American, and probably all male. The group has claimed credit for at least four bombings.

The size and composition of these groups is largely conjecture, because police and the FBI have been almost totally unsuccessful in attempts to infiltrate them with informers. An FBI informer named Larry Grathwohl managed to penetrate the Weatherman for six months beginning in late 1969, but no other undercover agent has ever managed to infiltrate any of the underground groups. Charles Bates, chief of the San Francisco FBI office, explains this failure by pointing out that with the exception of the Weather Underground, the groups are small, tightly knit, and deeply suspicious of strangers. The Weather Underground is just as tightly knit, is even more suspicious of strangers since its 1969 infiltration, and is divided into small cells of only about a half dozen members each. There is also the factor that the intelligence level of the leadership of the more dedicated revolutionary groups is much higher than that of the ordinary criminal gang.

The underground group which managed to inspire more headlines than any other during its short life span was the smallest of all in size, never exceeding a hard-core membership of more than a dozen at any one time, and it received the least support from aboveground radicals. The act that gave it the first headlines was condemned by radical leaders ranging from Angela Davis to Jane Fonda.

About seven o'clock on the evening of November 6, 1973, Oakland, California, school superintendent Marcus Foster, a black, and his white deputy, Robert Blackburn, were shot down by assassins on the parking lot of the school district's administration building. Foster was killed, Blackburn seriously wounded. The next day a communiqué was received by newspapers and radio and television stations in the Bay area from a previously unheard-of terrorist group calling itself the Symbionese Liberation Army Western Regional Youth Unit. It read:

SUBJECT: The Board of Education, The Implementation of the Internal Warfare Identification Computer System.

WARRANT ORDER: Execution by Cyanide Bullets. Date: November 6, 1973.

WARRANT ISSUED BY: The Court of the People.

CHARGES: Supporting and taking part in the forming and implementation of a Political Police Force operating within the Schools of the People. Supporting and taking part in the forming and implementation of Bio-Dossiers through The Forced Youth Identification Program. Supporting and taking part in the building of composite files for the Internal Warfare Identification Computer System.

TARGET: Dr. Marcus A. Foster, Superintendent, Oakland, California, Robert Blackburn, Deputy Superintendent, Oakland, California.

On the afore-stated date, elements of the United Federated Forces of the SLA did attack the Fascist Board of Education, Oakland, California, through the person of Dr. Marcus A. Foster, Superintendent of Schools, and Robert Blackburn, Deputy Superintendent.

This attack is to serve notice on the Board of Education and its Fascist elements that they have come to the attention of the SLA and the Court of the People and have been found guilty of supporting and taking part in crimes committed against the children and the life of the people.

The reference to cyanide bullets caused the police to accept the communiqué as authentic because it had not been released to the public that the bullets used in the crime had been tipped with the deadly poison potassium cyanide. It was assumed that the Forced Youth Identification Program reference concerned a grand-jury recommendation Foster had approved requiring junior- and senior-high-school students to carry identification cards as a method of reducing violence in the schools. However, in the face of parent protest, Foster had publicly withdrawn his support of the measure some days before he was murdered.

Two months later, on January 10, 1974, Joseph Remiro, 27, and Russell Little, 24, were stopped by police on a traffic matter in Concord, California, near Oakland. The suspects drew guns and a gun battle ensued, ending in the capture of both men. In their possession was found the weapon later established as the one that killed Marcus Foster. Subsequently the two were convicted of the murder.

Less than a month after the capture of Remiro and Little, on February 4, 1974, the SLA made worldwide headlines by kidnapping nineteen-year-old Patricia Campbell Hearst, granddaughter of the legendary newspaper publisher William Randolph Hearst, from the apartment in Berkeley she shared with her fiancé, Steven Weed. After badly beating Weed, the kidnappers dragged the screaming girl outside, threw her into the trunk of a car, and drove off.

The saga of Patty Hearst during the next nineteen months reads like the wildest of fiction, it is so implausible. The ransom demanded by the SLA was that the Hearst family pass out several million dollars' worth of food to the poor in the San Francisco area. There were also hints that the release of Remiro and Little might be demanded, but no definite demand of that was ever made. Patty's father, Randolph Hearst, with the assistance of the Hearst Foundation, a medical charity founded by the late William Randolph Hearst, met ransom demands, only to receive the shocking announcement from Patty via a tape recording that she had voluntarily decided to join the SLA and had taken the revolutionary name of Tania, after the mistress of the radical left's Latin-American revolutionary hero, Ché Guevara.

Then, on April 15, 1974, a black man and four white women wearing long black coats entered the Sunset Branch of Hibernia Bank in San Francisco, drew automatic carbines from beneath their coats, and ordered the two dozen customers and employees to lie facedown on the floor. Two of the women emptied cash drawers while the man and the other two women covered the people on the floor with guns. One of the women proudly announced, "We're from the SLA." Another, pointing to the armed young woman who had taken the central positon in the bank, said loudly, "This is Tania Hearst." The bandits escaped with nearly $11,000. As they left, the black man unnecessarily wounded two passersby by firing a burst through the glass door into the street, then fired at another innocent bystander after he got outside, but missed.

From bank cameras that had photographed all the bandits, they were identified as:

(1) Donald David DeFreeze, 30, self-styled "General Field Marshal" of the SLA, who had taken the revolutionary name Cinque, after the African black man who led a successful mutiny aboard a slave ship off the coast of Cuba in 1839. A habitual criminal classified by prison psychiatrists as "dangerous," he was serving his third prison sentence (five years to life for robbery and assault) when he escaped from Soledad Prison in March 1973. Prior to his transfer to Soledad, DeFreeze had been an inmate at

the California Medical Facility at Vacaville, a treatment center for mentally disturbed prisoners. There he joined an educational group called the Black Cultural Association, which held weekly meetings. Authorities permitted outsiders, most of whom turned out to be white middle-class radicals, to attend the meetings with the prisoners. There DeFreeze for the first time encountered the philosophy of revolution, and the seeds of the SLA were sown. After his escape, he sought refuge in San Francisco with Patricia Soltysik, one of the white radicals he had met at Vacaville. Five months later black convict Thero Wheeler escaped from Vacaville and was also given refuge by Soltysik, although his connection with the SLA, if any, seems to have been brief. The SLA was formed shortly afterward.

(2) Patricia (Mizmoon) Soltysik, 24, attended the University of California at Berkeley from 1970 to 1971, then dropped out to work as a janitor in the Berkeley Public Library. That one year was enough to interest her in radical causes. She changed her name to Mizmoon, not because it was her choice as a revolutionary name, but after Camilla Hall wrote a poem calling her that.

(3) Camilla Christine Hall, 29, the daughter of a Lutheran minister, graduated from the University of Minnesota in 1967. She worked as a social worker, first in Duluth, later in Minneapolis, before moving to Berkeley in 1970. There she met Patricia Soltysik and became interested in the same radical causes.

(4) Nancy Ling Perry, 27, had been a high-school cheerleader at Santa Rosa, California, and in 1964 supported conservative Republican Barry Goldwater's bid for President. Graduating from Berkeley in 1970, she started to work toward a master's degree in chemistry, but quit when her six-year marriage to black pianist Gilbert Scott

Perry broke up in 1973. After that she drifted from one job to another, including a stint as a topless blackjack dealer in a North Beach night club and another selling soft drinks at an outdoor stand. She was living with Remiro and Little in a rented house in Concord at the time of their arrest. Hearing the news on the radio, she phoned to alert William and Emily Harris, then unsuccessfully attempted to burn down the house before fleeing from it in advance of the arrival of the police. The attempted arson apparently was to destroy evidence that the house had been occupied by SLA members.

(5) Patricia Campbell Hearst.

In addition to Joseph Remiro and Russell Little, other members of the SLA at that time were:

(6) William (Cujo) Wolfe, 22, son of a Pennsylvania doctor. He attended the University of California at Berkeley in 1971 and 1972, where he became involved in student activism and took some black-culture courses. He was one of the white radicals who attended meetings of the Black Cultural Association at Vacaville. At the time Remiro and Little were arrested, Wolfe was visiting his parents in Pennsylvania. When he received a long-distance call the day after the arrests, he immediately disappeared.

(7) William Taylor Harris, 29, ex-Marine, with a master's degree in urban education from Indiana University, worked for the Berkeley post office. Harris had already been radicalized by his battle experience in Viet Nam before arriving in Berkeley, and was a member of the Viet Nam Veterans Against the War. When Nancy Ling Perry phoned the news of Remiro's and Little's arrests, he, his wife, and Angela Atwood, who lived with them, fled from their Oakland apartment so fast that they left a half-brewed pot of coffee on the stove.

(8) Emily Schwartz Harris, 27, wife of William Harris, was a graduate of Indiana University and a former junior-high-school teacher. At Berkeley she worked as a clerk-typist at the university and became deeply involved in campus radical activities.

(9) Angela Atwood, 25, met the Harrises at Indiana State University, where she majored in education, and went with them when they moved to Berkeley. She subsequently was married, but in June 1973 left her husband and moved in with the Harrises.

The next bizarre event in the saga occurred in May 1974, when William Harris, accompanied by his wife, was stopped outside a Los Angeles sporting-goods store by a clerk who had seen him shoplift a pair of socks. As the two men began to struggle, a woman seated in a Volkswagen van across the street, later alleged to be Patty Hearst, sprayed the upper part of the store with automatic fire from a carbine. That succeeded in making the clerk release Harris, and the three escaped in the van. Abandoning the van a short time later, the trio stole and abandoned three other vehicles during their flight, briefly kidnapping the eighteen-year-old male driver of one, but releasing him unharmed.

The following day, on a tip, police and FBI agents surrounded a house in a Los Angeles residential section. The blazing gun battle between the lawmen and the six members of the SLA in the house was televised live to the world. When the smoke cleared, the six SLA members were dead. They were Donald DeFreeze, Nancy Ling Perry, Patricia Soltysik, William Wolfe, Camilla Hall, and Angela Atwood.

Then, on September 18, 1975, Patricia Hearst's nineteen months with the SLA came to an end with her arrest and the simultaneous arrests of William and Emily Harris.

Another man and woman were also arrested, but they were subsequently cleared of complicity in the criminal activities of the SLA. The Harrises were indicted on eighteen counts each, ranging from bank robbery to murder. Patty was also indicted on several charges, and was first tried separately for the robbery of the Hibernia Bank. That sensational trial, taking place in San Francisco, was as much circus as trial. Flamboyant defense attorney F. Lee Bailey advanced the defense that Patty had been brainwashed, and put three psychiatrists on the stand to substantiate the claim. The prosecution countered with their own psychiatrists, who testified to the exact opposite of the defense experts. The exhibition did nothing for the image of psychiatry in the eyes of the general public. In a wry swipe at his colleagues, Thomas Szasz, professor of psychiatry at the State University of New York at Syracuse, wrote in the *New Republic* for March 6, 1976:

> What then, are the psychiatrists doing in the Hearst trial? They are "testifying" for whoever pays them. More than 300 years ago, an English aristocrat defined an ambassador as an honest man sent abroad to lie for his country. I would define a forensic psychiatrist as an honest doctor sent into court to lie for his masters.

The jury, possibly believing none of the psychiatrists and basing the decision on other evidence, found the defendant guilty. But such are the vagaries of our criminal-justice system that an alternate jurist, who had listened to all the evidence along with the regular jurists, wrote *Time* magazine that if she had been on the jury instead of being merely an alternate, she would never have permitted that verdict. The verdict is under appeal.

William and Emily Harris were tried in Los Angeles on charges of armed robbery, kidnapping, and auto theft stemming from the May 1974 sporting-goods store incident. Found guilty, on August 31, 1976, both were sentenced to 11 years to life imprisonment.

As bewildering to the average American as what converts well-brought-up young women into terrorists is the question of what they expect to accomplish by setting off bombs. The terrorist has a number of rationales. One is that acts of terrorism get the attention of the general public, whereupon revolutionary messages may be delivered. Another is that such acts will inevitably cause the authorities to overreact by repressing everyone's civil rights, and the counterreaction will be revolution. Jane Alpert was so convinced of this that she has said she confidently expected the revolution to take place within six months of the time she went underground in 1971.

The most interesting thing about the terrorist movement, insofar as this study is concerned, is that while women have been approaching equality with men in other fields of crime, this is the only one in which they have come to be dominant. There seems to be little doubt that they not only outnumber men in the predominantly white underground organizations, but run the shows. Despite Donald DeFreeze's grandiloquent title of "General Field Marshal," most observers feel he was merely a figurehead and that the women SLA members were in actual command. This is borne out by captured SLA documents in which the word "man" was repeatedly scratched through in order to substitute the word "woman." It is also borne out by the leaders of the largest revolutionary group, the Weather Underground, being now predominantly female, whereas it was almost totally male when the organization first went underground. In 1975 five leaders of the Weather Underground agreed to filmed interviews for a documentary film titled Underground, provided their faces were not shown. Three of the five were women.

The saddest thing about the entire movement is that these intelligent, well-educated women are pursuing a will-o'-the-wisp. The basic assumption of all terrorists is that when the existing corrupt "system" is destroyed, the good guys will take over. But the hard fact is that there are no good guys. Unfortunately, those most likely to rule benignly, humanitarians such as Albert Schweitzer or Martin Luther King, never aspire to political power. If the revolutionists get their way and actually manage to destroy the system, out of the ashes of American democracy a Joseph Stalin or an Adolf Hitler is much more likely to emerge.

Chapter 10

Women in Prison

Since men's and women's prisons have many things in common and many differences, we will first examine the United States prison system as a whole before concentrating on women's prisons.

In recent years there has been a good deal of rhetoric by law-and-order advocates about "crime in the streets." There has been criticism of "kid-glove" handling of hardened criminals by too-lenient judges, and clamor to clamp down on such criminals with higher conviction rates and stiffer sentences.

The facts are that the conviction rate for serious crimes is higher in the United States than anyplace else in the world from where records are available, our sentences are harsher, and our prisons and jails already bulge beyond their capacities.

There is, of course, much unsolved crime everywhere in the world. In the United States only 21 percent of the crimes reported to police during 1975 were solved. Most of the unsolved crimes were minor ones in the Part II group. The record of clearances of serious crimes against the person is much better. In 1975 police solved 78 percent of all homicides reported, 51 percent of all forcible rapes, 64 percent of all aggravated assaults, and 27 percent of all robberies. The clearance rate for serious crimes against property was below the general average, however. Only 18 percent of the reported burglaries, 20 percent of the larcency-thefts, and 14 percent of the motor-vehicle thefts were solved.

Criminals actually arrested hardly receive the pampered treatment that law-and-order advocates charge they receive. More than a million people are arrested on serious charges each year. About a third of these are cleared by police investigation and are released without any court action. The remainder go through the process of arraignment, which is a hearing before a judge during which they may enter a plea. If the plea is guilty, they may either have a sentencing date set or be sentenced right there.

If the plea is not guilty, a trial date will be set. Of these about another 110,000 have charges dropped by prosecuting attorneys after arraignment but prior to trial. The largest single reason why these cases are dropped is the refusal by complainants to continue to press charges, a matter for which neither the police nor the courts can be blamed. Of the remaining roughly 550,000, about 480,000 plead guilty, and only 70,000 go to trial. Of these about two thirds are convicted.

Nearly all of the guilty pleas are the result of so-called plea bargains, in which the prosecuting attorney agrees to reduce the charge in return for a guilty plea, thereby saving the time and cost of a trial. This procedure has come under vigorous attack from those who believe our judicial system is not harsh enough on criminals, but the fact is that if even one more criminal case out of ten went to trial, the entire system would creak to a halt because of the backlog of cases. In jurisdictions all over the country judges are already ordering numerous persons awaiting trial on criminal charges released because they have been sitting in jail so long that their constitutional right to speedy trial is deemed violated. In New York City alone some 200 felony cases *per day* are arraigned in a court open twenty-four hours a day, seven days a week.

One of the causes of our jammed courts is simply the adversary system, which pits defense lawyers against prosecuting attorneys in forensic duels. In the so-called civil-law nations of Europe the inquisitorial system is used in the courts. Under it the prosecutor, defense lawyer, and judge are all bound by ethical principle to seek out and reveal the truth of what actually happened, with the result that trials proceed much more quickly than in the United States. Under the adversary system trial is considered a contest between the prosecution and the defense, with the judge as a referee, rather than a cooperative search for the truth. The defense lawyer not only is not required to divulge any information that is damaging to his client's case, but would be regarded as either incompetent or unethical if he did. The result is that defense lawyers employ every legal technicality available and use every delaying tactic possible that they think may help their clients.

There is no evidence that the quality of justice in civil-law nations such as France is any lower than in common-law countries, and there is considerable evidence that it is faster, more certain, and less costly. Chief Justice of the United States Supreme Court Warren Burger has suggested a sutdy of the adversary system by the American Bar Association, with the goal of reforming its abuses, or perhaps even abolishing it in favor of the inquisitorial system.

A statistic that should be of interest to those who complain about our legal system being too soft on criminals emerges from the above data: of those prosecuted for serious crimes, 96 percent are convicted of at least something, and it is reasonable to assume that at least some of the 4 percent acquitted are actually innocent.

Though it is undoubtedly true that plea bargaining allows many guilty persons to escape with mere fines and/or probation in lieu of prison, it is also true that there is nowhere left to jam more prisoners. In 1975 Louisiana's Department of Corrections began contemplating bringing a World War II troopship out of mothballs to serve as a prison. In Florida, where there was no room for one third of the inmates, prisoners were living in army tents and converted warehouses. One dormitory designed for 90 had 170 crammed into it. In Georgia overcrowding became so impossible that Corrections Commissioner Allen Ault threw the problem into the laps of the courts by announcing that no new inmates would be accepted in any of the state's thirty-seven correctional facilities. In Virginia 2,000 state prisoners were being held in municipal and county jails because there was no room for them in state prisons. North Carolina prisons were packed 30 percent above capacity; Alabama prisons held 50 percent more than they were designed for. Less severe crowding, but still crowding existed in every other state and in the federal prisons.

For a country that accuses itself of coddling criminals, the United States spends an awful lot of money on prisons. According to the *Criminal Law Quarterly*, we jail more people per 100,000 of population than any other nation in the world from which reliable figures are available. Out of fifteen European and Western Hemisphere nations from which figures ranging from 1970 through 1972 were obtained, the Netherlands ranked lowest, with only 22 of each 100,000 of its subjects behind bars. The United States had 200. Poland was second, with 190, Australia had 128, Canada 90, England and Wales 81, France 61, and Japan 51. Spain, to which law-and-order advocates sometimes point as a nation where there is tough law enforcement, had only 40 per 100,000 of its citizens in jail, one fifth the United States rate.

The above figures comprise all jailed persons, including those awaiting trial. In the United States there are about 450,000 persons behind bars at any given moment, but only about 200,000 are in federal and state prisons. The rest are in local jails, where—except for state prisoners being held there because of lack of room in state prisons—they are either serving brief sentences for minor crimes, or are awaiting trial and are unable to raise bail. Of the 200,000 in state and federal prisons, only about 9,000 are women. Of the 250,000 in local jails, about 15,000 are women.

With all these people behind bars, there is widespread agreement among sociologists, law-enforcement leaders, the judiciary, and even among many of the people running the prisons that our whole prison system is a failure. Raymond K. Procunier, former director of the California Department of Corrections, said in a December 1974 interview with a staff writer for *U.S. News and World Report*:

Society's concepts about prisons make no sense at all. We're charged with conflicting responsibilities: keeping convicted felons away from the "good people" and, at the same time, in the unbelievably unnatural society that prevails in prison, rehabilitating them. You cannot send a man to San Quentin . . . and reasonably expect him to come out better than when he went in. . . . If there is any way to protect society without sending a criminal to prison, we should take that course. Long incarceration in big prisons should be reserved for high-risk offenders who cannot be safely controlled in other ways.

There is virtually total agreement among all authorities that certain dangerous criminals, such as mass murderers, should never be released on society. But there is sharp disagreement about who else should be behind bars, and what should be done to them while there. Many hold that no one who is not a threat to society should be imprisoned, regardless of the offense, and that imprisonment for such victimless crimes as narcotics use, gambling, and prostitution is both unjust to the prisoner and to society. Usually the same people who believe that feel also that prison authorities have no right to force "treatment" on such prisoners. As long ago as 1859, John Stuart Mill wrote in *On Liberty*:

> The principle is, that the sole end for which mankind are warranted, individually or collectively, in interfering with the liberty of action of any of their number is self-protection. That the only purpose for which power can be rightfully exercised over any member of a civilized community, against his will, is to prevent harm to others. His own good, either physical or moral, is not a sufficient warrant. He cannot rightfully be compelled to do or forbear because it will be better for him to do so, because it will make him happier, because, in the opinion of others, to do so would be wise, or even right. These are good reasons for remonstrating with him or reasoning with him, or persuading him, or entreating him, but not for compelling him, or visiting him with an evil in case he do otherwise. To justify that, the conduct from which it is desired to deter him must be calculated to produce evil to someone else.

The objection many modern theorists have to forced "treatment" is twofold: first, that it too often constitutes cruel and unusual punishment; and second, that it doesn't work. The theory that rehabilitation instead of punishment should be the goal of imprisonment is about a hundred years old and, until relatively recently, was one of the seldom questioned principles of penology. But now the questioners are in the majority. That the various treatments tried over the years, ranging from psychotherapy through aversion-drug programs and shock treatment to psychosurgery, do not reduce recidivism has been established by numerous studies. Sociologist Robert Martinson of the City College of New York reviewed *all* studies of correctional treatment since World War II and concluded that none of the various rehabilitative programs had any appreciable effect on the rate of recidivism of released convicts.

Statistics seem to bear this out. About 30 percent of all inmates released from federal and state prisons, both male and female, return to some prison. It is estimated that another 35 percent have further trouble with the law on a local level, and spend additional time in municipal and county jails. Thus the actual recidivism figure could be called 65 percent.

The charge that rehabilitative programs often constitute cruel and unusual punishment is based on the belief that the philosophy of rehabilitation has given prison personnel and parole boards unwarranted power over the lives of prisoners, and the human tendency is always to use unsupervised power harshly and unjustly. The villain is the indeterminate sentence, which gives prison authorities a weapon to force "treatment" on prisoners whether they want it or not, and places the future of each prisoner in the hands of a parole board. Most states have indeterminate sentences, which means that instead of a convicted criminal being sent to prison for a specific and definite period, the judge will give him both a minimum and a maximum term to serve, such as one to five years. It is then up to the parole board to decide when the offender has been sufficiently rehabilitated to merit release. Since the minimum and maximum terms often vary widely (in California second-degree burglary brings one to fifteen years, robbery five years to life) the convict is under powerful coercion to accept "treatment" when it is offered as a shortcut to parole, and furthermore is completely dependent on the parole board for his future prospects.

Such boards usually consist of a preponderance of retired law-enforcement officers and retired prison officials, simply because members are appointed by governors, and it is only natural for such persons to be considered as having the proper backgrounds for dealing with convicts. The net result is a sameness of parole boards throughout the country, with nearly all members believing in tight discipline. The power they wield over those who come before them is total, and is subject to no appeal. The convict's problem is not to become rehabilitated, but merely to convince the board that he is rehabilitated. When he has done as much time as the board deems appropriate to his particular offense, has undergone sufficient rehabilitative treatment, and is properly humble and spirit-broken when he appears before it, he will be granted parole. If he fails to make a good impression, he can try again a year later.

George Jackson, the black who was killed in a California prison during what authorities called an escape attempt, but which some of his supporters charged was deliberate murder, and whose prison letters were published in *Soledad Brother* in 1970, was one convict who refused to barter his self-respect for freedom, and consequently never got it. In one of his letters he wrote:

No one walks into the board room with his head up. This just isn't done. . . . If a man gets a parole from these prisons, Fay, it means that he crawled into that room. . . . No black will leave this place if he has any violence in his past, until they see that thing in his eyes. And you can't fake it, resignation-defeat, it must be stamped clearly across the face.

Currently there are some experiments underway designed to demonstrate that this dehumanizing process should be ended. The program being most closely watched by penologists is that of the new federal prison at Butner, North Carolina, which opened in May 1976 at a cost to the taxpayers of $13.8 million. When the Federal Bureau of Prisons ordered construction of the facility in 1969, it was to be called the Center for Behavioral Research. Later the name was changed to the Federal Center for Correctional Research. When it finally opened, it was simply called the Federal Prison at Butner.

The changes in name represented changes in penal philosophy while the facility was under construction. The original idea was to test various behavioral modification techniques on different groups of prisoners in an effort to find out which were most effective. *All* such techniques had been coming under increasing criticism from civil libertarians and from those concerned with prison reform, though, and there was strong objection from both sources to further research using nonvolunteer prisoners as guinea pigs. Federal Bureau of Prisons Director Norman Carlson therefore turned to psychiatrist Martin G. Groder to design a modified program, and also to serve as the first warden. Although Groder's plan sounded much more benign than the original, it was still research, and *any* behavioral-modification research was being regarded with increasing suspicion by civil libertarians and with increasing fear by the prisoners who would be the subjects. Carlson finally gave in to pressure and scuttled all plans for such research in favor of the theories of Norval Morris, dean of the University of Chicago Law School. In place of Groder, he appointed as the first warden Donald A. Deppe, former professor of philosophy at the University of Maryland and former director of education for all federal prisons.

Rehabilitation techniques at the new prison are based on the theories outlined by Norval Morris in his 1974 book *The Future of Imprisonment*, in which he proposed a "voluntary prison." Morris said prisons fail to rehabilitate because they try to cure criminal tendencies in such a degrading environment that nothing more than pretended cooperation from prisoners can be expected. Instead of "compulsory helping programs" he recommended that prisons require only that inmates endure their set sentences. Vocational training and other assistance, such as psychotherapy, should be available, but the choice to accept should be the prisoners'. Morris' theory was that such things help only prisoners who actually want them, and are useless for others.

There are 200 prisoners at Butner, all male, all eighteen or over, all still having one to three years to serve, and all in prison for at least the second time. Warden Deppe explains that repeaters were deliberately picked because "we want prisoners for our project who are not the most likely to succeed." The 200 were randomly picked from a list of 750 in the various federal prisons who met qualifications.

There are no gun towers, no cell blocks, and no barred windows at Butner, and each inmate has the key to his own 7½-by-9½ foot cell. Guards wear slacks and blazers instead of uniforms, and inmates may wear either their own clothing or comfortable coveralls furnished by the prison. It is still a maximum-security facility, though. The outer doors of the residence buildings are bolted at night, and the forty-acre complex has two 14-foot fences spaced twenty feet apart ringing it, both topped by barbed wire and equipped with electronic devices that signal if anyone tries to scale them. The space between the two fences is filled with coiled barbed wire.

Each of the 200 inmates goes through an orientation session during which he is told a definite date of release. It is explained that much of what he does meantime is up to him, and he learns that the traditional time off for good behavior is abolished. Since nothing he does can reduce his sentence, there is therefore no incentive to "act" rehabilitated in order to win a parole. He is offered elementary, high-school, or college courses for credit, vocational training, and counseling in such matters as alcoholism and drug addiction. But he is not required to accept any of these programs and even may be transferred to another prison after three months, if he so desires.

For each prisoner sent to Butner, another is randomly selected from inmates in other federal prisons who meet the same qualifications. These prisoners act as a control group, and both they and the Butner inmates will have follow-up studies made on them after their release from prison. Comparison of the rate of recidivism between the two groups will indicate the effectiveness of the Butner program. Obviously it will be years before any such data become meaningful, but meantime Warden Deppe hopes for a more immediate indication of success. He says: "If we can run an institution for these prisoners without intraprisoner predatory violence and in conditions of relative freedom within the prison, then we can do it for all prisons, if we want to."

Another experimental program, involving women only, has been conducted at the State Correctional Institution at Niantic, Connecticut, for several years. Here, too, the inmates have their individual rooms, with doors they may lock for privacy, and are allowed to wear their own clothing. One fourteen-inmate section of the prison has been designated the "moral development unit," and its residents live under a special set of rules. Within limits the fourteen are self-governing, setting their own rules and deciding what discipline is meted out to fellow inmates who violate the rules. The idea behind the program, which was devised by Lawrence Kohlberg, a social psychology professor at Harvard University, is to create a self-governing "just society" within the prison that will develop a strong-enough sense of morality within the inmates to prevent them from breaking the law again after they get out.

The inmates live according to a written contract with the staff, the terms of which have been previously agreed upon by both parties. Regular meetings jointly attended by both inmates and staff are held to discuss problems and mete out punishment to violators of the contract. Suggested punishments are voted on, and the majority prevails. Often punishments are written assignments similar to those given by elementary-school teachers to misbehaving pupils, such as an essay explaining why the offender committed the breach of contract and defining what her future behavior will be.

A 50 percent reduction in recidivism is claimed for the program, but critics point out that the study group is too small for meaningful statistics, and the subjects are not serious offenders. Most are in prison for drug-related crimes, and are such low-risk inmates that part of the program is to allow them three-day home paroles every sixty days. Nevertheless Connecticut correctional officials are so impressed by the program that a similar "moral development unit" has been established for men.

The first prison in the United States for women only was the Indiana Women's Prison, which was opened in 1873. Prior to that women were merely imprisoned in designated sections of male penitentiaries. That is still the situation for nearly half the women in prison, and for most in local jails. Of the two federal prisons to which women are sent, one is all female (the Federal Reformatory for Women at Alderson, West Virginia), the other (Terminal Island in California) is a predominantly male prison with a women's section. There are 28 state prisons for women, 24 other prisons with women's sections. Of the roughly 3,400 local jails in which women are authorized by local ordinance to be held, only about a half dozen are all-women facilities. The rest are merely separate cell blocks in facilities primarily designed for male inmates.

Most of these prisons and jails are a far cry from the moral development unit at Niantic. For the most part they are even more dehumanizing than male prisons. As a rule local jails are even worse than prisons. Often filthy and overcrowded, almost none have any programs of any sort other than work programs. Recreation, if any, seldom involves more than outdated magazines to read and controlled periods of television watching. The prisoners spend most of their time either sitting idle in cells, or performing such menial tasks as scrubbing floors.

The prisons are not a great deal better, although as a rule they are considerably cleaner. It is common practice for new female inmates to be placed in isolation for up to two weeks on arrival at the prison. After finally being allowed to join the regular prison population, they may be returned to the "hole" at any time for minor infractions of rules. A few years ago an inmate at the Pennsylvania State Correctional Institution for Women charged that she was placed in solitary confinement for four months merely for sneaking a bath in an officer's quarters instead of using the communal showers for prisoners.

The "hole" or the "bing" is usually a windowless cell with nothing in it but a mattress and a toilet. Sometimes there is not even a mattress. At the Colorado Women's Correctional Institution the three isolation cells are in a subbasement. Each has three solid walls and one barred wall. Two have toilets and mattresses. The third, for serious offenders, has nothing but an open drain in the floor. In all fairness it has to be said that the latter has not been used in recent years, but it is still there as a threat.

Vocational training and rehabilitation programs in many women's prisons or women's sections of male prisons are practically nil. When there are vocational training programs, they tend to be in traditional female fields, such as sewing classes. Inmates spend a good deal of time simply keeping the prisons clean. In some prisons they are allowed to work for wages, but the wages are very small. At the Federal Reformatory for Women there is a garment factory that makes uniforms for male federal prisoners and for the Veterans Administration. Pay runs around ten dollars a month.

About 75 percent of the adult women in prison have children, but many prisons bar visitors under sixteen, and even where children are allowed, visiting rights are usually very limited. Furthermore most women's prisons are in isolated areas difficult to get to without automobiles.

One common complaint by women inmates is that there

are too many petty and meaningless rules. At the
Pennsylvania State Correctional Institution for Women,
for instance, inmates are allowed six cigarettes a day and
are required to recite the Lord's Prayer in unison at bed-
time. Another common complaint is that they are treated
as mindless robots unable to think for themselves. Laura
Crites, who heads an Experimental Resource Center in
Washington, D. C., funded by the Department of Labor to
study the specific problems of female offenders, says: "In
general these places [women's prisons] just have a very
particular attitude toward women. They are looked upon
as children. They are not allowed to do any thinking on
their own. They are constantly referred to as 'girls' and are
treated that way."

Reformatories for girls are generally no better than adult
women's prisons. In his study Howard James found solitary confinement a common punishment for rule infractions. In one way he found the girls' institutions better
than those for boys. In the latter brutal treatment by
guards was common. Boys were flogged, were beaten with
hoe handles or rubber hoses, were slapped and kicked. At
the Ferris School for Boys in Delaware his discovery that a
number of inmates had punctured eardrums because
slapping was an officially approved method of discipline
brought about an investigation. Brutality was not evident
in girls' institutions he investigated, however—a difference he theorized might be because they were generally
run by women. Nevertheless most of the criticisms appli-
cable to adult women's prisons also applied to reformatories
for girls.

It is common for probation officers who work with
juveniles to feel the same sort of frustration as the judge
mentioned in Chapter 7, who had to commit a thirteen-
year-old girl to a training school because there was

nowhere else for her to go. Training schools are really juvenile prisons for the most part, with bars, locks, and all the demeaning rules and regulations found in adult prisons. Too often, as in the case of this thirteen-year-old girl, they are dumping grounds for problems no one else wants to handle. Also too often mere status offenders are mixed with experienced young criminals, who are only too willing to teach them criminal behavior. ("Status offender" is a term used by probation workers to designate juveniles who have been judged delinquent for certain offenses that would not be considered criminal behavior for adults.)

The dehumanizing effect of such places on youngsters was bluntly pointed out by Chief Judge David Bazelon of the United States District Court of Appeals for the District of Columbia in a speech to a group of judges:

> How do we treat our own children? We feed them, comfort them, play with them . . . and most of all warm them with our love and pride. Not many of us subject them to repeated batteries of tests and interviews, isolate them for weeks for misbehavior, make them account for every five minutes of their time, deny them privacy, censor their mail and refuse them all contact with the opposite sex. Yet in most systems this passes for treatment.

The National Council on Crime and Delinquency has issued this policy statement:

> Imprisonment of a status offender serves no humanitarian or rehabilitative purpose. It is, instead, unwarranted punishment, unjust because it is disproportionate to the harm done by the child's non-criminal behavior.

Milton Luger, President of the National Association of State Juvenile Delinquency Program Administrators, says:

With the exception of a relatively few youths, it would be better for all concerned if young delinquents were not detected, apprehended, or institutionalized. Too many of them get worse in our care.

George F. McGrath, head of the New York City Correctional System, says: "Correctional agencies contribute enormously to the crime rate."

A member of the Illinois Youth Commission suggested a drastic solution to the problem. He said the best answer was to bulldoze all reform schools to the ground.

That suggestion was probably whimsical. Just as there are dangerous adult criminals against whom society has a right to be protected, there are also dangerous juvenile criminals. And until such time as the problem of juvenile crime has been solved in some other way, society has a clear right to insist on the isolation of its dangerous members, regardless of their ages. Even if all abuses within the juvenile justice system are eventually reformed, there will probably still be a need for some type of institution for hard-core juvenile criminals.

In its 1967 report the President's Commission on Law Enforcement and the Administration of Justice urged correctional authorities to "develop more extensive community programs providing special, intensive treatment as an alternative to institutionalization for both juvenile and adult offenders." What the commission had in mind was intensely supervised probation programs in which offenders continued to live at home or in foster homes in their own communities, in lieu of the traditional probation program in which the average offender saw his or her probation officer for about ten minutes once a month, and halfway houses for those deemed in need of more intensive supervision. The suggestion was greeted with wide approval, but whenever authorities tried to implement such a program anywhere except in ghetto areas, there was strong resistance from homeowners. The average suburbanite applauded the philosophy until confronted with the prospect of having a halfway house in his community. Then he started organizing protest meetings.

In December 1975 Robert Vinter, George Downs, and John Hall of the University of Michigan's National Assessment of Juvenile Corrections Program issued a preliminary report on a federally funded study they were making of residential programs for juvenile delinquents. They found that despite evidence that such programs were both less costly and more effective than state institutions, only 17 percent of juvenile offenders were being placed in them. Although the study showed that there was "widespread interest" in such programs, only Massachusetts, South Dakota, Minnesota, and Utah sent as many as half their juvenile offenders to them instead of to state training schools and camps. Six states had no community-based programs at all.

It costs the fifty states about $300 million a year to support an average of somewhat fewer than 30,000 juveniles in prisons euphemistically labeled "training schools." It costs them about an additional $30 million to maintain a little less than 6,000 juveniles in community-based programs. Simple arithmetic shows that the cost of the latter is exactly one half the cost of the former per offender.

Associate Professor of Sociology Barbara Carter of Federal City College in Washington, D. C., discovered a rather touching custom among the inmates of some girls' reformatories during a study she was making. The girls often developed foster-kin relationships within the institutions, identifying certain older girls as their "mothers" or "aunts" and friends their own age as "sisters" and "cousins." The older girls so chosen seemed to find some kind of emotional need fulfilled also by their acquisition of "daughters" and "nieces," over whom they exercised a sort of maternal protectiveness against other inmates and staff members. This yearning for some sort of family was particularly marked among girls who had grown up in foster homes and had no real family background.

Chapter 11

Conclusions

Because, in my opinion, the increasing rate of female criminality is tied so closely to the increasing freedom being won by women, the most likely future prospect I can see is that female criminality will continue to increase until it eventually at least approximates the rate of male criminality. This opinion is based on the assumption that women will continue to become increasingly liberated, but that seems to be a reasonable assumption. The fact that women put up with their second-class status for so many centuries has little bearing on the speed with which further changes in the male-female relationship may take place. Once freedom has been tasted, the hunger for more is not likely to be appeased by tokenism. Concessions merely tend to increase demands.

This is something the unoppressed never seem to be able to grasp when an oppressed group first begins to demand its rights. "Give them an inch and they want a mile" is a common indignant reaction of the "haves" after generously making a minor concession to the "have-nots" only to be met with clamor for more concessions instead of being thanked.

About a dozen years ago, when the Black Muslim movement was just starting to gain strength, I attended a public forum at which a Black Muslim leader explained the philosophy behind the movement. During the question-and-answer period afterward, a white member of the audience asked the speaker if he didn't feel obliged to concede that blacks had made considerable progress in civil rights. The speaker said, "If I thrust a sword into your chest clear up to the hilt, then pulled it out so that only about a foot of steel was sticking in you, would that make you feel better about it?"

His point, of course, was that blacks were never going to be content with mere improvement in their status; they wanted absolute equality with whites. Like popcorn, a little freedom always incites hunger for more. It is quite possible for oppressed people to become so resigned to their fate that they cease struggling against it so long as they see no hope of improvement. Blacks and women both remained resigned to their fate for centuries. But once the realization that freedom was possible had appeared, neither was likely to accept less than complete freedom. Mere "improvement" wasn't enough.

Traditionalists, male and female both, lament the privileges women will have to forfeit in return for full equality. Opponents of the proposed Equal Rights Amendment to the United States Constitution seem to have temporarily stalled its ratification by trumpeting the sacredness of these privileges. Won't women have to give up alimony if ERA passes, for instance, and won't America's sweethearts, wives, and daughters be dragged into the armed forces on an equal basis with men? Won't chivalry die?

If the death of chivalry means that women will have to get along without the traditional courtesies men have offered them in place of rights, most feminists will say good riddance. But there is a little more to chivalry than mere courtesy. It also involves a protective attitude toward women, which unquestionably has given them over the ages an advantage over men in some ways. One of them is that in the past women have usually not been held nearly so accountable for their crimes as men.

There is little statistical evidence, either in support of or against the belief, that chivalry has an important effect today on the number of women being arrested and imprisoned, but there is ample evidence that it had marked impact in the past. A legal as well as a social double standard has been traditional in the United States until relatively recently, as it has been traditional in almost all civilizations throughout history. In the United States it was felt by those who made the laws (mainly men) that a fair balance was being struck because though women had less legal protection than men in some areas, they made up for it by being granted more protection in others. Thus the pre-World-War-I denial of property rights and voting rights for women was justified on the grounds that they received much compensating protection to make up for this lack of rights. Women were exempt from military draft, and labor laws limited the hours they could be worked and the job hazards they could be exposed to. There was the common-law principle that held men accountable for family support but excused women from such responsibility, and the judicial tendency to grant women custody of children almost automatically in divorce cases. Furthermore, alimony was available to women but not to men. As recently as 1948 the United States Supreme Court gave its blessing to this legal double standard when Justice Felix Frankfurter wrote the majority opinion in *Geosart v. Cleary*, a case challenging a

Michigan statute that forbade any female to act as a bartender unless "she be the wife or daughter of the male owner of a licensed liquor establishment.":

> The fact that women may now have achieved the virtues that men have long claimed as their prerogatives and now indulge in vices that men have long practiced does not preclude the states from drawing a sharp line between the sexes, certainly in such matters as the regulation of liquor traffic.

In illustration of how much judicial thinking in this area changed during the next quarter century, the same court's decision in the 1973 case of *Frontiero v. Richardson* read in part:

> There can be no doubt that our nation has had a long and unfortunate history of sex discrimination. Traditionally, such discrimination was rationalized by an attitude of "romantic paternalism" which, in practical effect, put women not on a pedestal, but in a cage.

In the past this "romantic paternalism" carried over to the treatment of women before the bar of justice. In *Commentaries on the Law of England* Blackstone touched on the principle of "presumed coercion," which held women guiltless who had helped their husbands commit crimes because it was assumed they had merely obeyed their husbands' commands.

Somewhat similar thinking, although hardly as drastically one-sided, was apparent at the trial described in Chapter 3 of stagecoach robber Pearl Hart. Although she and Joe Boot were equal partners in the crime, her jury found her innocent, while poor Joe's found him guilty. It was also apparent in the theories of William Isaac Thomas, quoted in Chapter 4 as writing: ". . . man is

merciless to woman from the standpoint of personal behavior, yet he exempts her from anything in the way of
contractual morality, or views her defections in this regard with allowance and even with amusement."

All things change, though. If "romantic paternalism"
still has an effect on how women are treated within the
criminal-justice system, it isn't apparent from available
statistics. If anything, statistics seem to indicate that
women are treated slightly worse than men. Though they
are arrested for only about 20 percent of serious crimes
committed, women constitute between 22 and 23 percent
of the prison population. They are arrested for about 15
percent of the Part II crimes, but constitute between 16
and 17 percent of the population of local jails. This
suggests either that fewer women than men receive probation instead of prison sentences, or that their prison sentences are longer. There are indications that both are the
case.

A large number of prisoners in local jails are simply
awaiting trial and are unable to make bail. Suspecting sex
discrimination in bail matters, in 1972 an organization
called the Citizens' Council for Criminal Justice made a
study of bail-bond records in the District of Columbia.
When they discovered a much higher percentage of
women than men were required to post bond instead of
being released on their own recognizance, they polled
judges and bail officials for the reason for the disparity. It
turned out that there was a general feeling, unverified by
any actual data, that women posed a "higher risk of flight"
than men. Thus, in that locality at least, a disproportionate number of women were in jail simply because of an
unsubstantiated belief among male officials that women
are less trustworthy than men.

One explanation for the percentage of women in prison

being slightly higher than their arrest rate would seem to warrant may be because sentences tend to be longer for women than for men committing the same types of crimes. Logically this would result in a higher percentage of women being in prison at any given moment, simply because many were still there who would have been back in society if their sentences had been equivalent to those handed out to men. A half dozen states where indeterminate sentences have been abolished for men still retain them for women. Not too long ago there were eight, but state supreme courts recently overturned the laws in two states as discriminatory. The probability is that all will eventually be overturned, either by state supreme courts or by the United States Supreme Court.

The Pennsylvania Muncy Act of 1964 stipulated:

> . . . any female . . . convicted for a crime punishable by imprisonment for more than a year must be sentenced to confinement in the State Industrial Home for Women and the sentence shall be merely a general one . . . and [the sentence] shall not fix or limit the duration thereof.

The effect of the act was to require that women convicted of crimes punishable by more than one year had to be sentenced to the maximum term allowable by law, whereas men could receive lower sentences. In a 1967 test case titled the *Commonwealth of Pennsylvania v. Daniels*, a Pennsylvania superior court actually upheld the constitutionality of this blatant sex discrimination, but the following year its decision was reversed by the state supreme court with these words:

> There is no reasonable and justifiable difference of deterrent between men and women which would justify a man being eligible for a shorter maximum prison sentence than a woman for the commission of the same crime.

In 1971 the New Jersey supreme court reviewed a case involving a woman convicted of bookmaking. Although the court noted that under New Jersey's indeterminate sentencing law the defendant could be held in prison for as long as five years, whereas a man convicted of the same offense could not be sentenced to more than two years, in the *State of New Jersey v. Costello* it upheld the law with this curious reasoning:

> . . . the legislature could legitimately conclude that female criminals were basically different from male criminals, that they were more amenable and responsive to rehabilitation and reform . . . which might, however, require a longer period of confinement in a different type of institution.

In less legalistic terms what the court was saying was that because women respond better to rehabilitation efforts than men do (a value judgment totally unsupported by any investigative data), there was justification for keeping them in jail longer. The fact that rehabilitative programs in women's prisons were virtually nonexistent went unnoted by the court.

Fortunately in 1973 the same New Jersey supreme court struck down the act permitting this sex discrimination as violative of the constitutional guarantee of equal protection under the law.

There seems to be some evidence, or at least some very strong opinions, that chivalry still plays an important part in the treatment of female offenders up until the time judges hand out sentences. In *Sisters in Crime* Adler says:

> The deferential treatment of females begins with the arresting officer, positioned as the link between society and the criminal-justice system, and extends throughout the process of arraignment, hearing, trial and sentencing. Sometimes these differences serve the women well and some-

times ill, but they always serve the criminal-justice system poorly. In the ordinary course of events, police tend to handle the minor offenses of young girls unofficially in order to spare them the social stigma associated with court appearance. It is not considered prestigious and may even lower a patrolman's or male detective's status to arrest a woman.... Long experience has taught frustrated prosecutors the difficulties involved in achieving convictions for women who are free of previous social stigmatization. Even the pursuit of such a conviction can be a source of embarrassment because judges and juries share a similar disinclination to find women offenders guilty. In the United States, as well as in other countries, courtroom chivalry has time and again resulted in decisions for acquittal which were more faithful to accepted attitudes than accepted evidence.

Yet in *The Criminality of Women* Pollak presented convincing data to show that in the case of violent crimes the rate of conviction was higher for women than for men. The total evidence seems to indicate that women have much less chance of being arrested for minor crimes, or of being sentenced to jail if convicted of them, but have more chance of both arrest and conviction for violent crimes, and generally serve longer sentences for them than men do. Perhaps this is because male chivalry, though willing to view minor infractions of the law by women "with allowance and even with amusement," becomes outrage when "unladylike" crimes are committed by women.

The problem of female criminality cannot be separated from the problem of criminality in general. The solution of the former is inextricably bound to the solution of the latter. The urgent goals are to reduce *all* crime, repair our ailing criminal-justice system, and to empty our prisons of all but dangerous criminals.

The standard solution to crime advanced by virtually all sociologists as the best one is to correct the inequities in our society that breed criminals. There is little question that such social reforms as converting ghettos into livable residential communities and giving ghetto residents equal opportunity to enjoy the material benefits of our affluent society would drastically reduce crime. But from the cynical viewpoint of realism, there are more votes in a large defense budget than in social-welfare programs, and it seems unlikely that unless there is a violent revolution, any vast transfer of wealth from the rich to the poor will take place in the foreseeable future. Since violent revolution seems equally unlikely, despite the wistful hopes of the underground terrorists, it is only pragmatic to look for more realizable solutions, even though any solutions other than social change have to be essentially stopgap.

One persistent suggestion from many sources as a method of reducing prison population is either to legalize or decriminalize certain behavior now classified as criminal. (Legalization means removing all restrictions; decriminalization merely removes criminal penalties without denoting official approval, and usually substitutes civil penalties such as small fines, which are handled administratively as infractions, much in the same way traffic offenses are handled in most places.) The "victimless crimes" advocates want to see either legalized or decriminalized include prostitution, gambling, marijuana and narcotics use, presently proscribed sexual behavior between consenting adults, drunkenness, distribution of pornography, status offenses of juveniles, and such vaguely defined offenses as loitering and vagrancy. Some of the arguments are good, some unconvincing.

One of the unconvincing arguments was presented at a seminar on women in prison that I attended while researching this book. One of the panelists, a woman lawyer who was a militant feminist, made the startling statement that decriminalization of prostitution would release half the women jailed in the United States, because "between fifty and seventy percent of the women in jails are committed for prostitution, vagrancy, or loitering, and some sixty percent of the women in prison for felonies were first arrested for prostitution."

My research disclosed that this was totally false. The fact is that though a large number of women in prison are prostitutes, *none of them* is there for prostitution only. Prostitution is only a misdemeanor in forty-nine states (in Nevada it is legal), and conviction never draws a prison sentence unless other crimes are involved too. Few convicted prostitutes even serve jail sentences of any appreciable length, most sentences being merely small fines. When jail sentences are given, they usually run from 3 to 10 days, with an occasional sentence of from 30 to 90 days for repeating offenders. It is true, as the woman panelist indicated, that a large proportion of women in prison are prostitutes, but they are there for other crimes. A California probation officer told me that though a large number of her cases during the two and a half years she had been on the job had been prostitutes, all were on probation for offenses other than prostitution, such as narcotics use or rolling customers. In two and a half years she had *never had a single case of prostitution only*, simply because sentences for that offense were too minor to include probation.

There may be other arguments for legalizing or decriminalizing prostitution, but the concept that either would release large numbers of women from behind bars is pure fantasy.

There is a better argument for the decriminalization of marijuana. Prior to a 1975 California law that made possession of less than one ounce an infraction punishable by only a small fine, 50 percent of the criminal cases tried in Los Angeles were for narcotics possession, use, or sale, most involving marijuana. A number of other states have passed similar laws, but there are still large numbers of young people in prisons for periods ranging up to twenty years for possession of amounts of marijuana that would bring only fines of $20 to $500 in the states where possession has been decriminalized. Aside from the obvious injustice of this, it uselessly crowds our prisons.

Though more and more authorities, including jurists and law-enforcement officials, are coming around to the opinion that marijuana possession should at least be decriminalized, the majority opinion on hard drugs such as heroin swings the other way. But regardless of moral views on the subject, or the conviction of most law-enforcement officials that hard drugs have visited a terrible evil on society, it is impossible to escape the conclusion that prison sentences have done nothing to solve the drug problem in this country. In fact, many authorities believe they increase the crime rate by throwing countless young people whose only brushes with the law involved narcotics into contact with hardened criminals who steer them into more serious crime.

My own feeling is that while I believe the legalization, or even the decriminalization of hard drugs would create serious social problems, the present system of incarceration has created equally serious social problems of another sort. Some kind of medical approach to the matter would seem wiser, perhaps a program of required treatment of addicts under supervision in institutions without bars or walls, such as halfway houses. Virtually any solution other than throwing addicts in prison would seem wiser, particularly since it is common knowledge that narcotics are almost as easily available behind bars as on the street. And it is undeniable that clearing all narcotics offenders from our prisons would drastically reduce the prison population.

The National Council on Crime and Delinquency set up a subunit called the National Advisory Commission on Criminal Justice and Goals, which has made a number of specific suggestions on how to reduce both crime and the prison population. It believes in the abolition of indeterminate sentences, the establishment of maximum sentences of 5 years for most offenses, and up to 25 years for dangerous criminals, those convicted of a third felony, and certain felons classified as "professional criminals." Without actually calling for the legalization or decriminalization of "victimless" crimes, it recommends the "diverting" of these offenders from the criminal-justice system into other avenues of correction, such as counseling, medical and mental-health services, job training, and job placement. One of its strongest recommendations is to continue the trend away from confining offenders who pose no danger to society in institutions in favor of community-based programs. The eventual goal of such a program would be to retain only a small number of maximum-security prisons for dangerous criminals who must remain isolated from society, and to sentence all others merely to closely supervised probation, combined with meaningful rehabilitative programs in their own communities.

A number of other organizations have made similar studies and have recommended ways to reduce the prison population. Just to mention two, there is the National Task Force on Higher Education and Criminal Justice, and the Justice Office of the Unitarian-Universalist Service Committee. Some of the numerous recommendations made by these and other organizations include:

(1) An educational program to make people aware of the legal consequences of criminal acts, and of their constitutional rights if arrested.

(2) Negotiation of warrants, an experimental program sponsored by the American Mediation Association in only two cities so far. It is designed to mediate disputes between parties where one has filed a criminal complaint against the other, in an attempt to get the complaint withdrawn and the dispute settled in some other way.

(3) Wider use of release on recognizance in lieu of bail. Studies show that failure to appear is no higher for accused persons released on their own recognizance while awaiting trial than for those who posted bond. They also indicate that judges are more likely to grant probation instead of giving prison sentences to persons who are not in confinement when they appear in court, presumably because their very appearance as agreed demonstrates a sense of responsibility.

(4) Pretrial "diversion" to rehabilitative programs of various kinds. In this procedure charges are dropped if the accused agrees to treatment. The program has been used in numerous localities with good results for alcohol-related offenses. Typically the offender escapes a criminal charge by agreeing to join Alcoholics Anonymous or to enroll in some other rehabilitative program for problem drinkers.

(5) Halfway houses, which include a wide variety of residential and out-patient treatment centers for everything from mental problems to drug addiction in local communities. Some of these are government run, others privately funded.

(6) Restitution, a system under which offenders who have stolen or damaged property are required to repay the victims instead of going to jail. Such orders may be col-

lected in the same manner as any other court judgment if the offenders are unable or unwilling to pay—that is, wages may be garnisheed or liens may be attached against property owned by the offenders.

(7) Sentences to perform community service for public and private welfare organizations in lieu of going to jail.

(8) Weekend sentences, where minor offenders are allowed to continue working at their jobs and report to the jail each weekend until they have served their full sentence in two-day spans.

Whatever solutions are eventually adopted, they are bound to be better than our present system of warehousing criminals for certain periods, then thrusting them back into society unimproved and frequently embittered. But they are also bound to bring criticism. A great many people feel that the primary purpose of prison is punishment, and they are going to be dissatisfied with any program that they feel "coddles" criminals instead of increasing the harshness of their punishment. That a 65 percent recidivism rate pretty conclusively demonstrates that punishment fails to deter crime is ignored by such critics, who continue to decry the "country-club atmosphere" of prisons and to demand that criminals "learn their lessons." Unfortunately the main lesson they learn is how to be more hardened criminals when they come out than they were when they went in.

A matter that every honest citizen should muse upon before he decides what in his opinion should be done to persons while they are in prison is that more than 99 percent of them, including those repeatedly convicted of violent crimes such as armed robbery, rape, and murder, are eventually released on society. No rhetoric demanding that they be locked up forever is going to change that chilling statistic. "Life" sentences in all states mean eventual parole for all except a few special prisoners, such as mass murderer Charles Manson. In some states parole from murder sentences is possible within eighteen months. Since we are going to have to live with these released prisoners in our communities, it is only good sense to adopt some system best designed to prevent them from becoming repeaters.

Bibliography

Alder, Freda, Sisters in Crime: The Rise of the New Female Criminal. New York, McGraw-Hill, 1975.

Baldwin, James, The Fire Next Time. New York, Dial Press, 1963.

Beauvoir, Simone de, The Second Sex. New York, Random House, 1974 (orig. pub. 1953).

Blackstone, William, Commentaries on the Laws of England. Dobbs Ferry, N.Y., Oceana Publications, 1966 (orig. pub. 1765–1769).

Cowie, John, Cowie, Valerie, and Slater, Eliot, Delinquency in Girls. Atlantic Highlands, N.J., Humanities Press, 1968.

De Rham, Edith, How Could She Do That? New York, Clarkson N. Potter, 1969.

Freud, Sigmund, New Introductory Lectures on Psychoanalysis. New York, W.W. Norton, 1965 (orig. pub. 1933).

Friedan, Betty, The Feminine Mystique. New York, W.W. Norton, 1974 (orig. pub. 1963).

Giallombardo, Rose, The Social World of Imprisoned Girls. New York, John Wiley & Sons, 1974.

Glueck, Sheldon and Eleanor, *Five Hundred Delinquent Women*. Millwood, N.J. Kraus Reprint Co., 1934.

Greer, Germaine, *The Female Eunuch*. New York, McGraw-Hill, 1971.

Heaps, Willard A., *Assassination: A Special Kind of Murder*. New York, Hawthorn Books, 1969.

Jackson, George, *Soledad Brother: The Prison Letters of George Jackson*. New York, Coward, McCann & Geoghegan, 1970.

Jackson, Joseph Henry, *Bad Company*. New York, Harcourt Brace Jovanovich, 1949.

Jacobs, Harold, *Weatherman*. Palo Alto, Calif., Ramparts Press, 1971.

James, Howard, *Children in Trouble: A National Scandal*. New York, David McKay, 1970.

Kagan, Jerome and Howard A. Moss, *Birth to Maturity: A Study in Psychological Development*. New York, John Wiley & Sons, 1962.

Keniston, Kenneth, *Youth and Dissent: The Rise of the New Opposition*. New York, Harcourt Brace Jovanovich, 1971.

Konopka, Gisela, *The Adolescent Girl in Conflict*. Englewood Cliffs, N.J., Prentice-Hall, 1966.

Lasch, Christopher, *The New Radicalism in America 1889–1963: The Intellectual as a Social Type*. New York, Alfred A. Knopf, 1965.

Lombroso, Cesare, *The Female Offender*. New York, Appleton-Century, 1920 (trans. from the Italian, orig. pub. 1903).

Mead, Margaret, *Male and Female*. New York, William Morrow, 1975 (orig. pub. 1949).

Mead, Margaret, *Sex and Temperament in Three Primitive Societies*. New York, William Morrow, 1963 (orig. pub. 1935).

Mill, John Stuart, *On Liberty*. New York, W.W. Norton, 1975 (orig. pub. 1859).

Morris, Norval, *The Future of Imprisonment*. Chicago, University of Chicago Press, 1974.

Mulvihill, Donald J., Melvin M. Tumin, and Lynn A. Curtis, *Crimes of Violence: A Staff Report Submitted to the National Commission on the Causes and Prevention of Violence*. Vols 12 & 13, Washington, D.C., U.S. Govt. Printing Office, Dec. 1969.

Platt, Anthony M., *The Child Savers: The Invention of Delinquency*. Chicago, University of Chicago Press, 1969.

Pollak, Otto, *The Criminality of Women*. Cranbury, N.J., A.S. Barnes, 1961 (orig. pub. 1950).

Reckless, Walter and Barbara Kay, "The Female Offender" (A section of the *Report of the President's Commission on Law Enforcement and the Administration of Justice*.) Washington, D.C., U.S. Govt. Printing Office, 1967.

Roughhead, William, *Murderer's Companion*. New York, Press of the Reader's Club, 1941.

Smith, Pauline C., *The End of the Line*. Cranbury, N.J., A.S. Barnes, 1970.

Sparrow, Gerald, *Women Who Murder*. London, Abelard-Schuman, 1970.

Sussmann, Frederick B. and Frederic S. Baum, *Law of Juvenile Delinquency*. Dobbs Ferry, New York, Oceana Publications, 1968.

Sutherland, Edwin H. and Donald Cressey, *Principles of Criminology*. New York, J.B. Lippincott, 1966.

Thomas, William Isaac, *Sex and Society: Studies in the Social Psychology of Sex*. New York, Arno Press, 1974 (orig. pub. 1907).

————,*The Unadjusted Girl: With Cases and Standpoint*

for Behavior Analysis. New York, Harper and Row, 1970 (orig. pub. 1923).

Uniform Crime Reports for the United States. Washington, D.C., U.S. Govt. Printing Office, 1976.

Vedder, Clyde and Dora Somerville, *The Delinquent Girl.* Springfield, Ill., Charles C. Thomas, 1975 (orig. pub. 1970).

Whitehead, Don, *Journey Into Crime.* New York, Random House, 1960.

Index